STRANGER FACES
Namwali Serpell

**TRANSIT
BOOKS**

Published by Transit Books
2301 Telegraph Avenue, Oakland, California 94612
www.transitbooks.org

Copyright © Namwali Serpell, 2020
ISBN: 978-1-945492-43-3 (paperback) | 978-1-945492-47-1 (ebook)
LIBRARY OF CONGRESS CONTROL NUMBER: 2020009997

COVER DESIGN
Anna Morrison

TYPESETTING
Justin Carder

DISTRIBUTED BY
Consortium Book Sales & Distribution
(800) 283-3572 | cbsd.com

Printed in the United States of America

9 8 7 6 5 4

for Emily Brenes and Mike Isaac

INTRODUCTION

LOOK AT ME

I know. You can't. Well, I suppose you could search my name online. If we've met before, you could picture me. If we haven't, you could conjure me. Or maybe I'm with you, reading these words to you in some distant future. But let's say you read those familiar words, absent my presence. *Look at me*. What comes to mind?

For me, this three-word sentence has some assumptions built into it. One is that by *me*, I mean *my face*. Why? There is a great deal more to me than my face, which is one of the few parts of me that I can't actually see without a reflection or a recording. When I think or say the words *I* or *me*, I rarely picture my own face. So why is the face the seat of identity? What is it about the face—be it from the point of view of biology, neurology, psychology, philosophy, anthropology— that yields that cliché "the eyes are the windows to the soul"? In any case, *look at me* seems to equal *look at my face*.

Built into that instruction are also some assumptions about the nature of that face. It's presumably visible, close enough to see, uncovered, recognizable *as* a face, and impenetrable—we generally don't say *look into me* or *look through me*. To look *into* a face (searchingly) or *through* it (distractedly) would be either to go too far or not far enough in terms of seeing it. When it comes to dimension, this picture of the face corresponds to somewhere roughly between a filmic close-up and a passport photo. It is implicitly a direct view of the front of the head, not a view from the side or of the back. Another strangeness: is the front of the face really more legible than, say, the silhouette? We use both for mug shots, after all.

Embedded even deeper in the phrase *look at me* are assumptions about the situation in which it would be uttered. The grammar dictates a human speaker, a human listener, and a human face subjected to the view of functioning human eyes. You wouldn't say *look at me* to yourself or even to a mirror. We imagine a personal encounter between two people who know each other well enough for it to pass between them in a conversation. *Look at me* feels urgent, emotional. Prefaced by *please*, it becomes an appeal; by *I said*, it becomes an order. Between lovers, it's a call to intimacy, a promise of honesty. Between enemies, it's a threat of violence, a demand to be heard. *Look at me* vibrates with a sense of what we owe each other, that is, with a sense of ethics.

Doesn't this preclude some entities from that sense of ethical obligation? The very fact of an instruction between two humans also assumes that they are both alive and that their faces are capable of actions—speaking and looking, respectively—and expressions of feeling. But you might not say this sentence to a blind person, a victim of paralysis, or an animal.

The notion that human faces are recognizable, categorizable, and distinct from other kinds of faces first emerged as a scientific concept in Darwin's *The Expression of the Emotions in Man and Animals* (1872). Nowadays, facial recognition is a well-studied developmental stage in babies. Neuroscientists have located a part of the brain, the "fusiform face area," that lights up when we look at faces. For many, the face is the basis for sympathy, which is defined as "an affinity between certain things, by virtue of which they are similarly . . . affected by the same influence." The idea that morality is enhanced by face-to-face interaction has been promulgated by scientists since Darwin and can be summed up by the title of a 2001 article in the *Journal of Consciousness Studies*, "Empathy needs a face."[1]

The Jewish philosopher Emmanuel Levinas claimed that "the face *is meaning* all by itself."[2] In his work, he extols all the features I describe above: "the very uprightness of the face, its upright exposure, without defense. The skin of the face is that which stays most naked, most destitute. It is the most naked, though with a decent nudity." He presumes a human face, a frontal view of the face, and a kind of complete or replete meaning in it: "the face signifies itself"; "the face is meaning all by itself." This face is adamantly not an object; it resists exchange and conversion.[3] For Levinas, it's not just sympathy with a face that promotes ethics. The face also subjects us to a sense of radical, unique otherness, what he calls *alterity*. The face shocks us into recognizing our stark difference from, and our profound responsibility for, one other.

In sum, the face—what we ask each other to engage with when we say *look at me*—is fundamental to how we understand ourselves. The face means identity, truth, feeling, beauty, authenticity, humanity. It underlies our beliefs about what constitutes a human, how we relate emotionally, what is pleasing to the eye, and how we ought to treat each other. All of this—ontology, affect, aesthetics, ethics—rests on a specific version or image of the face. We might call it The Ideal Face. This book aims to break it.

I am by no means the first to try to take apart this picture of the face. What interests me is in fact the co-existence of these two opposed traditions: our continued belief in The Ideal Face and our persistent desire to dismantle it. Perhaps this just means that the face is an ideal before which we continually fall short. But I think we actually take pleasure in failed faces. The history of literature and art is littered not just with The Ideal Face but also with *stranger faces*, by which I mean both *strange faces* and the *faces of strangers*. The essays in this book take up a range of recalcitrant or unruly faces: the disabled face, the racially ambiguous face, the dead face, the faces we see in objects, the animal face, the blank face, and the digital face.

FIGURE, FETISH, ART

Stranger Faces probes our mythology of the face by treating it not as an ideal, but as a kind of sign—a symbol, a medium, a piece of language. A sign is made up of two parts: the *sign* itself—like a mark on a page or a spoken word—and whatever the sign refers to, its *referent*—a meaning, a concept, a person. The face is similarly divided, between the surface of the face itself and whatever we think that surface means: beauty, depth, a particular emotion, humanity.

When Levinas claims that "the face signifies itself" and "the face is meaning all by itself," he is suggesting that the surface and the meaning are fused, inseparable. I disagree. We know that signs don't always mean what they say. Signs can cease to point to referents because of willful acts of deception, distortion, or erasure. In fact, this potential disjunction between signs and referents is built in, a fundamental principle of language—and of faces, too. Studies have shown that the average person correctly assesses another person's expressions (thinking, agreeing, confused, concentrating, interested, disagreeing) only 54% of the time. Despite the belief that a face is clearer than a word, there's more variation in what facial expressions mean across culture, gender, and individuals than we might imagine.

A face is a *figure*. If the face is always split in two—a surface and a depth or a sign and its referent—then the stranger faces I consider intensify this disjunction. They are hard to *read* because they intensely distort the assumed correspondence between the surface and its meaning. They're too big or too dead or too blank or too fungible or too beastly; they don't conform. What they show us, I think, is that faces don't have to be human, in front of us, undamaged, whole, visible, beautiful, or recognizable at all. In fact, we seem to prefer thinking about them, playing with them, when they're *not*.

Stranger faces lead us to go beyond the usual question— *what should a face be?*—to an even more basic one: *what counts as a face and why?* If we dislodge The Ideal Face from its seat of power, the array of stranger faces we're left with might give us insight into faces as such, as we experience them. We might move toward new models of being, aesthetics, affect, and ethics that rely not on identity or truth, but on *pleasure*, in all of its richness and complexity. We might even traverse that ultimate taboo: treating the face as a kind of *thing*.

Stranger faces attract and repel recognition. They ride the line of legibility, and compel us to read them even though we know we are doomed to fail. I think we compensate for that failure by taking unexpected pleasure in it. The gap between the face and its depths is a span across which we fondle, flirt with, and fret over meaning. Room for error is room for play. In psychoanalysis, this pleasurable compensation is called disavowal. As Octave Mannoni said, "I know very well, but nevertheless,"[4] or applied here: "I know I can't read this face but nevertheless I try, and take pleasure in the effort." A more familiar word for this is fetishism.

The fetish has roots in anthropology and Marxist thought

as well as psychoanalysis. In all three realms of knowledge, the fetish describes when something is lost or absent—our relationship to a god, to the conditions of production, or to an imagined phallus—and a significant object is recruited to stand in or make up for that loss or absence. So, a shiny statuette, an idol, stands in for a god; the shine of a commodity conceals the labor that produced it; the shine on a nose sparks arousal in a fetishist who associates it with a penis. (It is no coincidence that this, Freud's first example of the fetish, is a kind of face-play.) Fetishistic pleasure is neither pure nor unequivocally positive. Indeed, fetishism is perverse by definition—it entails finding something good about what we assume to be bad: failure, absence, loss. It is complex, sometimes painful. But it is also an aesthetic relationship to the world.[5]

While the cross-cultural history of art is dominated by the face, we still assume that to treat a face aesthetically is to objectify it. To fetishize the face might seem to contravene not just Levinas's interdiction against treating it as currency but also an older one against "using people." Kant claimed that a person "is never to be used merely as a means for someone (even for God) without at the same time being himself an end."[6] This idea appears now in warnings against "objectifying" other people. Nonfictional and fictional accounts of rape, slavery, and genocide often point to dehumanizing others—treating them like machines or animals or as a means to an end—as the first step to harming them.

As psychology professor Paul Bloom put it in a 2017 *New Yorker* essay: "The thesis that viewing others as objects or animals enables our very worst conduct would seem to explain a great deal. Yet there's reason to think that it's almost the opposite of the truth." When you apply basic logic to, say, the practice of taunting people, you can see that "to believe that such taunts are effective is to assume that their targets would be ashamed to be thought of that way—which implies that, at some level, you think of them as people after all." In *Down Girl*, philosopher Kate Manne makes an analogous point about misogyny: "people may know full well that those they treat in brutally degrading and inhuman ways are fellow human beings, underneath a more or less thin veneer of false consciousness." Bloom concludes: "The aggressions licensed by moral entitlement, the veneer of bad faith: those things are evident in a wide range of phenomena, from slaveholders' religion-tinctured justifications to the Nazi bureaucrats' squeamishness about naming the activity they were organizing, neither of which would have been necessary if the oppressors were really convinced that their victims were beasts."[7]

If cruelty doesn't require dehumanization, nor does dehumanization require cruelty. Bloom raises the usefulness of a surgeon's clinical, unbiased view of a body. In her masterful study, *Persons and Things*, Barbara Johnson contests Kant's rule about not using people with another psychoanalytic concept, one that has a lot in common with the fetish—the "transitional object," like a teddy bear or a blanket, which is often personified and survives the child's efforts to destroy it. It thus teaches the child consistency and humility. Even beyond sadomasochism, many valuable and ethical relationships depend on this oscillation between a person and a thing. I would add to them the complex pleasures—dangerous, but not necessarily unethical—of treating the human face with the attention and value we grant to a work of art.

LOOK AT ME

Jennifer Egan's 2001 novel, *Look at Me*, begins: "After the accident, I became less visible. I don't mean in the obvious sense that I went to fewer parties and retreated from general view. Or not just that. I mean that after the accident, I became more difficult to see."[8] The narrator, Charlotte, flashes back to explain: driving without a seatbelt, she hits the brakes and "bursts through the windshield into the open air," breaking her ribs, arm, and leg, shattering every bone in her face:

My face was in the midst of what he called a "golden time," before the "grotesque swelling" would set in. If he operated immediately, he could get a jump on my "gross asymmetry"—namely the disconnection of my cheekbones from my upper skull and of my lower jaw from my "midface." I had no idea where I was or what had happened to me. My face was numb, I saw with slurry double vision and had an odd sensation around my mouth as if my upper and lower teeth were out of whack.[9]

She undergoes twelve hours of surgery, which she describes in detail: "eighty titanium screws were implanted in the crushed bones of my face to connect and hold them together . . . I'd been sliced from ear to ear over the crown of my head so Dr. Fabermann could peel down the skin from my forehead and reattach my cheekbones to my upper skull; . . . incisions were made inside my mouth so that he could connect my lower and upper jaws."[10]

Egan taps into a longstanding fascination with cosmetic surgery in journalistic accounts, from the report on Indian rhinoplasty published in *The Gentleman's Magazine* in 1794 to Alice Hine's recent deep dive in the May 2019 issue of *New York Magazine* into the new subculture of extreme facial surgery among "involuntarily celibate men." These "incels" are turning to the scalpel to achieve what they perceive to be "'manlier' noses and head shapes" like "a wide jaw or prominent brow" or "angular 'male model' cheekbones."[11] Egan's aesthetic luxuriation over medical details is also characteristic of fictional narratives that depict facial surgery—novels like Thomas Pynchon's *V.* (1963) and films like Georges Franju's *Les yeux sans visage* (1960), Scott McGhee's and David Siegel's *Suture* (1983), Alejandro Amenàbar's *Abre los ojos* (1997), and Pedro Almodóvar's *La piel que habito* (2011). Works like *Phantom of the Opera* luxuriate through layering: the addition of a mask that stands in for the face, competes with the face, implies that the face is itself constructed and removable. It seems one way we compensate for a perceived injury to or deficiency in a face is to aestheticize its repair.

Indeed, the strange thing about Charlotte's face in *Look at Me* is that it's of greatest aesthetic interest when it's shattered and when it's being reconstituted: "My face was just entering the 'angry healing phase': black bruises extending down to my chest, the whites of my eyes a monstrous red; a swollen, basketball-sized head with stitches across the crown"; "rather than fading . . . my bruises simply changed color, like fireworks whose finale won't arrive."[12]

Perhaps even stranger is that though Charlotte's surgery is successful—seamless—it makes her unrecognizable. Her face is unscarred, still beautiful, possibly improved by plastic surgery, but somehow *vague*. Once a professional model—the title is obviously riffing on this valence of *look at me*, too—she can't return to her work: "people looked at me in the particular way people do inside the fashion world: a quick ravenous glance that demands beauty or power as its immediate reward. And then they looked away, as if what they had seen were not just unfamiliar, but without possibility."[13] Her accident has destroyed what she calls "a shadow self" or "shadow face": "that caricature that clings to each of us, revealing itself in odd moments when we laugh or fall still, staring brazenly from certain bad photographs."[14] Her face no longer functions as a source of identity, power, or ethical relation for her.

For Egan, the opposite of The Ideal Face isn't the non-ideal face—what I'm calling "the stranger face." It is the face "without possibility," which our glances pass over as if over porcelain, or through as if through glass. And outside of Egan's novel, *that face doesn't exist*. Its very impossibility is what makes the premise of *Look at Me* so intriguing. Every *real* face is interesting, worth looking at, often precisely because of its deviation from an abstract ideal. If we think of *every* face, even the strangest one, as a work of art, then beauty and truth—what we claim to seek when we look at a face, what we want to hear when we say *look at me, what do you see?*—suddenly seem insufficient indices for all that a face can hold, for all it can do.

I am a mixed-race woman who has been mistaken for Chinese, Dominican, Egyptian, Eritrean, Ethiopian, Mexican, Somali, Spanish, and Thai. My face has been compared to E.T. (big eyes), to a mango (asymmetrical), and to Cleopatra (¯_(ツ)_/¯). Zambians often tell me I look like my mother, who had much darker skin than I but the same bone structure; Americans, who see skin color first, don't catch the likeness. Men on the street have called me beautiful and ugly, at about the same frequency. If I say *look at me*, I frankly don't know what you'll see.

Maybe you'll picture a meme. The 2013 movie, *Captain Phillips,* stars Tom Hanks—the coziest face that ever sat on a screen—as the titular captain. When Somali pirates board his cargo ship, their leader Abduwali Muse (played by Barkhad

Abdi) points at his own eyes and says, "Look at me. *Look at me*. I'm the captain now." The intensity of this interracial encounter and the deft performance by the previously unknown Abdi, make it a perfect meme. Hanks's Hollywood smile and squinty affability contrast sharply with Abdi's imperfect teeth and big eyes, which widen between the two commands: *look at me*. I recently tweeted a fictive riff on this meme:

Namwali Serpell
@namwalien

Me: Look at me

Unassuming date: What?

Me: LOOK at me

Unassuming date: *looks at me*

Me: I'm the captain now

9:24 PM · Sep 14, 2019 · Twitter Web App

The joke has layers of race and gender built into it: Hanks's face hovers over my unassuming date's; my face over Abdi's. This is what fascinates me about faces—not their ideality but their mutability, the way they shift and layer, always abrim with charged relation.

They remind me of how art works. Art, like everything, is entangled with capital. But it isn't limited to it. While Kant argued against objectifying people, he also argued that the beauty of art itself is not a means to an end, that it does not satisfy desires, but is rather "purposive without purpose" ("final without end," in some translations).[15] Art isn't just a commodity, an object to be bought and sold, in order to satiate some craving; it's a creation and an experience. It moves, and it moves us. It is this fugitive aspect of the face as art—its fleeting, fleeing quality, the sense that it is always turning into, or toward, or away from—that I hope to evoke in these pages.

1.

ELEPHANTS

IN

ROOMS

DISFIGURE

Dear Sir,

I am writing to you about a man in our hospital. He needs your help. His name is Joseph Merrick, and he is 27 years old. He is not ill, but he cannot go out of the hospital because he is very, very ugly. Nobody likes to look at him, and some people are afraid of him. We call him the 'Elephant Man.'

—"A Letter to the Editor," *The Times*, December 4, 1886[16]

Went to the London Hospital, where as President I received at 5 o'clock the Prince and Princess of Wales, who came to open the new home just finished for the Nurses of the Hospital. We passed through the wards, saw the unfortunate man called the elephant man, who is a painful sight to look at, though intelligent in himself, and then I read an address to the Prince and Princess to which the Prince replied.

—Diary of the Duke of Cambridge, May 21, 1887[17]

. . . At 3 came the Duke. He gave H.R.H. an account . . . of the Princess of Wales . . . at the London Hospital, tearing up her bouquet, to give a flower of it to each sick child & each sick woman. Of their having seen the Elephant-man, poor creature—a sad spectacle! *enormous*, with two great bosses on the forehead really like an elephant's head, & a protruding face like a snout, one *enormous* hand like the foot of an elephant, the other, the left hand, extraordinarily, exceptionally *small*! He can never go out, he is mobbed so, & lives therefore a prisoner; he is less disgusting to see than might be, because he is such a gentle, kindly man, poor thing!

—Journal of Lady Geraldine Somerset, aide to the Duchess of Cambridge, May 22, 1887[18]

"Nobody likes to look at him." "A painful sight to look at." "A sad spectacle." The adjectives, raised up by hyperbole or under a thin line of erasure: "ugly," "poor," "enormous," "disgusting." We can't know what it would be like to look at Joseph Merrick now. Perhaps political hindsight would open our eyes or our minds so as to perceive his intelligence, gentleness, kindness first. The latest of the seemingly endless renditions of his life—a play scripted by the Australian Tom

Wright—has Merrick uttering this line: "I am the most extraordinary thing in this city, yet when you look at me you don't see me."[19] And yet even this play looks at Joseph Merrick and sees *The Real and Imagined History of the Elephant Man*.

Why do we still use that moniker, The Elephant Man? From our vantage point over a hundred and fifty years later, it almost has the rhythm of inevitability to it. But if we were to see one of the famous pictures of him now, without context, would we stumble upon that name? Where did it come from? One story goes that the symptoms of Merrick's condition—diagnosed at various points during and after his life as Proteus syndrome, Maffuci syndrome, Albright's disease, von Recklinghausen disease, and neurofibromatosis, but yet to be pinpointed, even with our latest DNA technology—physically resembled an elephant. Rough wrinkled skin covered Merrick's neck, face, and leg; the limbs on his right side were uniformly thick; and the protuberances of his brow—"those great bosses"—hung forward over his face "like a trunk."

In a three-page pamphlet entitled "The Autobiography of Joseph Carey Merrick," and likely co-written with showman Tom Norman, in whose penny gaff shop Merrick was exhibited, we find what is meant to be the official story:

I first saw the light on the 5th of August, 1860, I was born in Lee Street, Wharf Street, Leicester. The deformity which I am now exhibiting was caused by my mother being frightened by an Elephant; my mother was going along the street when a procession of Animals were passing by, there was a terrible crush of people to see them, and unfortunately she was pushed under the Elephant's feet, which frightened her very much; this occurring during a time of pregnancy was the cause of my deformity.

The measurement around my head is 36 inches, there is a large substance of flesh at the back as large as a breakfast cup, the other part in a manner of speaking is like hills and valleys, all lumped together, while the face is such a sight that no one could describe it. The right hand is almost the size and shape of an Elephant's foreleg, measuring 12 inches round the wrist and 5 inches round one of the fingers; the other hand and arm is no larger than that of a girl ten years of age, although it is well proportioned. My feet and legs are covered with thick lumpy skin, also my body, like that of an Elephant, and almost the same colour, in fact, no one would believe until they saw it, that such a thing could exist. It was not perceived much at birth, but began to develop itself when at the age of 5 years.[20]

Merrick's stage name doesn't pretend to be literal, the way a comic-book Spider Man or a circus Snake Woman might. The Elephant Man is a *figure* in many senses: a delineation of a body and face; a representation or shape; a figure of speech, a piece of language used in a nonliteral sense.

This last definition frays into two more possibilities: a metaphor or a metonym. A metaphor is based on *similarity*, so when we say "The White House whitewashed the story," the verb is a metaphor—cleaning up a story resembles white-washing flaws in a wall. A metonym is based on *association*, in the way that the White House refers to the people who work there, not the physical building itself. The Elephant Man is both: a metaphoric similarity to the animal (its physical features) and a metonymic association with the animal (his mother's accident with an elephant).

The idea of maternal impression—that a pregnant woman's experiences in the world will affect, or *impress* upon, the child in her womb—has a long history. It is already a combination of metaphor and metonym: the baby comes to *resemble* something, whatever it has come into mediated contact with. It's a familiar logic of contagion, or mirroring. An x-ray vision: the elephant's head in profile facing a protu-berant belly; the baby's head behind the veils of skin and flesh, facing back, shifting, morphing to resemble it. As this vision hints, though, this figure makes sense only through a great semantic leap; the size, look, and biology of a man and an elephant couldn't be more distinct.

In his memoir, *The Elephant Man and Other Reminiscences,* the surgeon and anatomist Frederick Treves begins his depic-tion of Merrick by describing a "life-size portrait" painted in "primitive colors":

This very crude production depicted a frightful creature that could only have been possible in a nightmare. It was the figure of a man with the characteristics of an elephant. The transfiguration was still more of the man than the beast. The fact—that it was still human—was the most repellant attribute of the creature. There was nothing about it of the pitiableness of the misshapenned or the deformed, nothing of the grotesqueness of the freak, but merely the loathsome insinuation of a man being changed into an animal.[21]

Treves' account suggests that there is something monstrous about a half-transformation, a stalled metamorphosis. It's as if Merrick were the embodiment of Dr. Jekyll caught midway through his transformation into the hirsute, bestial, racialized, queered, and "deformed" Hyde.

The Elephant Man is what Akiri Mizuta Lippit calls an *animetaphor*.[22] It both points to and elides the elephant, which appears not as a mere idea or abstraction, but as a hovering material presence. The Elephant Man conjoins seemingly incompatible beings, conjuring a wondrous, ungainly hybrid, like a minotaur, a chimera. The presence of two nouns is important; they didn't call him The Elephant, or The Elephantine Man. Elephant and Man sit in an uneasy balance, the relative heft of the two creatures perpetually offset by the relative semantic weight of their significance. In short, which is the *heavier* term? More than a figure, The

Elephant Man is almost a *disfigure*, a piece of language that works even though it shouldn't.

In classical rhetoric, the term *catachresis* refers to an error in spelling, pronunciation, or grammar—like a malapropism. It comes from the Greek word for "abuse," and scholars like Jacques Derrida and Paul de Man applied the term more broadly to refer to all failures of figuration—like mixed, strained, or paradoxical metaphors. De Man's analysis of *prosopopoeia*, the rhetorical act of "putting a face to a thing" or making an object speak, offers two examples that both feel like catachresis: the "face of a mountain or the eye of a hurricane." The critic Tilottama Rajan says catachresis is the eruption of something "monstrous"; it is a mixed, hybrid form that abuses words and confuses substances; it can "dismember the texture of reality and reassemble it in the most capricious of ways"; "it is a prosthesis that grafts a body back onto the nonhuman" or "an *upsurge* of the human in the nonhuman."[23] This is again the horror of a half-transformation. If metaphor is etymologically to carry over, a catachresis is a halted journey.

The distorted language that Merrick's contemporaries used about him evinces all of the features of catachresis that Rajan describes: eruption, monstrosity, hybridity, abuse, confusion, dismemberment, reassemblage, caprice, admixture, prosthesis, graft, the nonhuman. Take the jumbled panoply of thing-like qualities Treves attributes to Merrick's face:

From the intensified painting in the street I had imagined the Elephant Man to be of gigantic size. This, however, was a little man below the average height and made to look shorter by the bowing of his back. The most striking feature about him was his enormous and misshapened head. From the brow there projected a huge bony mass like a loaf, while from the back of the head hung a bag of spongy, fungous-looking skin, the surface of which was comparable to a brown cauliflower. On the top of the skull were a few long lank hairs. The osseus growth on the forehead almost occluded one eye. The circumference of the head was no less than that of the man's waist. From the upper jaw there projected another mass of bone. It protruded from the mouth like a pink stump, turning the upper lip inside out and making of the mouth a mere slobbering aperture. This growth from the jaw had been so exaggerated in the painting as to appear to be a rudimentary trunk or tusk. The nose was merely a lump of flesh, only recognizable as a nose from its position. The face was no more capable of expression than a block of gnarled wood.[24]

Treves presents this unveiling in terms of its incompatibility with previous images. "In the course of my profession," he says, "I had come upon lamentable deformities of the face due to injury or disease, as well as mutilations and contortions of the body depending upon like causes; but at no time had

I met with such a degraded or perverted version of a human being as this lone figure displayed."[25] Treves almost reenacts this for the reader by giving us that "very crude portrait" first, the nightmarish horror of which still pales in comparison to the real deal.

But despite all the protestation about Merrick's incomparable deformities, the passage *proliferates* with comparison: to bread, fungus, cauliflower, a stump, a lump, a block of gnarled wood. Later Treves again invokes the horror of the stalled metamorphosis, in the simultaneity of *before* and *after* in Merrick's arms: one is vegetal and animal, "overgrown with pendent masses of the same cauliflower-like skin" with "a fin or a paddle rather than a hand"; the other is "not only normal but, moreover, a delicately shaped limb covered with fine skin and provided with a beautiful hand any woman might have envied."[26] It's as if, confronted with the polar opposite to The Ideal Face—asymmetrical, inexpressive, disproportionate (that circumference "no less than that of a man's waist"); bumpy, uneven, rough; with an occluded eye, a nose only legible for its position, and enormous brows— Treves' mind lurches about, latching onto a dozen incomplete approximations.

Merrick can't be captured because he is splayed across several binaries—race, ability, gender (with his "beautiful hand any woman might have envied"). He epitomizes an ambivalence about legibility central to our relationship to all faces. Like beauty, strangeness compels a slew of metaphors whose very profusion indexes their ultimate failure. *Shall I compare thee . . . ?/ Thou art more . . .*

In the scandalized descriptions of Merrick with which I began, we find an analogous double imperative: *Don't look! / Look!* (The etymology of "monster" is *monstrum* or warning.) So the letter to the *Times* that claims "nobody liked to look at him" goes on to recount a contravening anecdote: "Merrick came back to London by himself. Everybody on the train and ship looked at him and laughed at him." For the elite of Cambridge, Merrick is "painful to look at," "a sad spectacle," but he "can never go out, he is mobbed so." Treves says that "everyone he met confronted him with a look of horror and disgust" but notes that when he was in public, "an eager mob . . . would run ahead to get a look at him." Treves later sums this up: "never could he be free from that ring of curious eyes or from those whispers of fright and aversion."[27] This maps onto the gestalt switch between horror and fascination.

That switch suggests a certain degree of relativity. Indeed, from our current point of view, it is not Merrick but the images his contemporaries used about him—animal, vegetable, mineral—that are "painful to look at." To compare a human to the nonhuman feels cruel, debasing, and connected to the physical abuse Merrick suffered.[28] But it's important to remember, per Paul Bloom, that cruelty doesn't require dehumanization. And Merrick himself held onto that strange moniker, The Elephant Man, and seems to have treasured the maternal impression origin story of his mother and the elephant. The illegibility of Joseph Merrick's face—its resistance to our usual categories of understanding—is what spurs all of these figures and stories about him. What if we chose *not* to treat Merrick's non-ideal face as a problem that stumps our aesthetic, affective, and ethical beliefs? What if, instead, we chose to think of it as a work of art?

SMILING DISEASE

On a gray, spitting day in Venice this past summer, I spent a morning strolling through the main exhibits of the Venice Biennale in the Arsenal. The building is tall and narrow, concrete and stolid, and like the cars of a train, you move from one enclosure to the next through a small vestibule. I turned one such corner and confronted a field of impaled skulls—of a kind. They were untouchable, behind an ankle-high rope, but you could circle them to an extent, see them in the round. Wooden branches, about as high and thick as broomsticks, were implanted in rough concrete blocks, heavy sacks nestled here and there at the base to keep them upright. And topping them were masks, or again, *skulls*—three-dimensional, chaotic conglomerations of long stringy hair, gnarled and carved wood, and clusters of metal nails like Congolese Nkondi.

The title of the exhibit was *Smiling Disease*. The placard told me that an American sculptor named Cameron Jamie designed this 2008 installation and commissioned an Austrian craftsman to make it. It riffs, the placard said, on the folk tradition of the Perchten, "an Alpine winter character associated with the Krampus," a subject of Jamie's earlier work, but it also "references the collections of tribal artefacts that were popular among Surrealist artists in the early twentieth century, thought to reflect contemporary ideas about the subconscious and the universal significance of dreams."

The ethnographic impulse that spurred Surrealism to break free of the cage of "realism" in the early twentieth century dovetailed with a psychoanalytic tendency to relegate the subconscious to the realm of the "primitive." Here is a characteristic conflation from Freud's essay on the uncanny: "It seems as if each one of us has been through a phase of individual development corresponding to this animistic stage in primitive men . . . everything which now strikes us as 'uncanny' fulfils the condition of touching those residues of animistic mental activity within us."[29]

Smiling Disease invokes what the West continues to associate with tribalism—the primitive, the raw, the regressive, the nightmarish realm of the Id. It also directs us to consider the longstanding conditions of contact zones: the contested, racialized idea of appropriation; the distortions of what counts as "ethnic"; the relative imbalance of labor between the "artist" who commissions and the "craftsman" who makes. These are scarecrows and upended brooms—with their Western fairytale, Oz-like associations—but they are also impaled heads. Like those that Kurtz displays in Joseph

Conrad's *Heart of Darkness*, they reinforce the stereotypes of "tribal savagery"; work as a mirror for the white imperialist "gone native"; and stage a dramatic critique of imperialism and its savage dismemberments.

But it has always struck me that this appropriation/expropriation of "tribal artefacts"—African, Oceanic, and Native American masks and sculptures, to be specific—is too often relegated to a plagiaristic crime rather than seen as a profound aesthetic influence. What if Western art's impulse was not to *escape* the real but to recognize modes of perception *more attuned* to the real? Duchamp's and Picasso's later experiments with Cubism didn't just take from these artifacts a connotation of savagery or subconscious desires. They also took the use of imbricated and faceted planes to convey dimension, torsion, perspective, and movement—a sculptural version of stop-motion photography that non-Western cultures had long been practicing. This is why the faces in *Smiling Disease*—and they are clearly faces—ask not just to be looked at, but to be walked *around*.

All this history hangs in the air as you circumnavigate the field of skulls, yet there is a curiously quotidian feel to the installation. Some of the faces are playful, with splayed teeth and jutting tongues; others are bestial, the hair horse- or goat-like, yet still humanoid. They escape attributions of gender and—"ethnic" or "tribal" flavor notwithstanding—of race. Texture is more crucial to their skin than color. The nails hammered into some of them warn us away (*monstrum*) but also gesture toward injury. But it's unclear, as in the work of Francis Bacon or Phoebe Boswell, whether it is injury or movement or a roiling centrifugal force that distorts them. Animal, vegetable, mineral. Figures, things, creatures, half-transformed.

The placard calls them "grotesque," but I think Mikhail Bakhtin's concept of the "carnivalesque" is more apt, in the sense of a masquerade that bursts with forms and media, that overturns binaries and hierarchies. The faces approach the sublime insofar as they are of the natural world and difficult to conceptualize; they approach the uncanny insofar as they are both homely and creepy. But they suit none of these aesthetic categories exactly—their hybridity has me reaching for a term that would capture the *pleasures* of monstrosity, of an eruptive catachresis.

And in this, they remind me of Joseph Merrick. This may seem outrageous. Joseph Merrick was a human being. But so was Cleopatra. What if we framed his face—with its multidimensional, multifaceted, multitextural complexity—in the terms with which we frame hers—as a myth, an icon, a loaded figure, so to speak? The Elephant Man's fame is often attributed to the profundity of his condition, by which I mean both how profoundly it changed his body and how its seeming contrast with his personality struck many as profound. But many other humans in history have embodied those profundities. Joseph Merrick is famous because he has long been an object of artistic representation.

The tradition of *displaying* The Elephant Man seems to have originated with Merrick himself. Having been cast out by his family after his mother's death, then banned from his job as a hawker, Merrick entered the Leicester Union Workhouse at age 17. After a few miserable years and a surgery that mitigated some of his physical discomfort, Merrick contacted a well-known showman, Samuel Torr, to propose himself as an exhibit. Torr soon passed Merrick onto Tom Norman, who always insisted that Merrick expressed his preference for the life of the "freak show" over that of both the workhouse ("I don't ever want to go back to that place," Merrick said) and, though he ended up there, the London hospital: "I was stripped naked and felt like an animal in a cattle market."[30] Norman's choice to display Merrick, and Treves's choice to describe that display through a double mediation—a portrait that gives way to a *tableau vivant*—in fact followed the trend of Merrick's own choice to be exhibited publicly.

The profusion of wild figures in descriptions of Merrick in his time—including his three-page Autobiography—is a small-scale version of the proliferation of artworks about him since his passing. There are at least five biographies of Merrick, several plays, and two films—David Lynch's 1980 production, starring John Hurt, did much to bring Merrick's story to public awareness. Merrick has become recognizable *in* his strangeness—indeed, it has become something of an honor to play him on film or on stage. Hurt was nominated for an Academy Award. Bradley Cooper was nominated for a Tony.

A couple of years ago, I went to see the London production of Bernard Pomerance's play in which Cooper starred.[31] I hadn't read the play, or much about it, so I experienced firsthand the remarkable *tromp d'oeil* Pomerance insists upon. Scene 3, titled "Who Has Seen the Like of This?" opens with a spotlight on Cooper, dressed only in boxers, as the actor playing Treves stands beside him and describes Merrick's body, a kind of perverse blazon. As succinctly described in the stage directions: "Treves *lectures*. Merrick *contorts himself to approximate projected slides of the real Merrick*."[32] Amazingly, this works. With no prostheses, only a slow, willful, visibly painful contortion of the actor's body, The Elephant Man comes to life.[33] We "see" him. Yet this vision is partial, or rather, hybrid, a live catachresis. Cooper maintains his posture for the rest of the play but he hovers inside or over Merrick, his physical beauty present in its distortion. This stages both the half-transformed quality of Merrick himself and the partial way we imagine when we experience art.

There's also something of Brecht's "alienation effect" to this—the idea that theater ought to prevent us from total immersion and emotional release by reminding us that the stage, the play, the actors are all part of an illusion.[34] Rather than showing us props or stage lights, here we are continually made aware of the actor's performance—and its inevitable *inadequacy.* It fails to be the bodily "failure" that many considered Merrick to be. This is because we know what Merrick looked like; his famously strange face becomes the "ideal" no actor can match. Pomerance's Introductory Note insists:

> Merrick's face was so deformed he could not express any
> speech at all . . . Any attempt to reproduce his appearance
> and his speech naturalistically—*if* it were possible—would
> seem to me not only counterproductive, but, the more
> remarkably successful, the more distracting from the play.
> For how he appeared, let slide projections suffice.[35]

I don't think we even need slides anymore.

So often has Merrick been depicted that, again like
Cleopatra, his representation—our shared conjured picture
of him—has eclipsed him. The recent discovery of a coin
bearing Cleopatra's profile attests that her reported beauty
has overtaken her historical face. As our standards have shift-
ed, our image of "the most beautiful woman in the world"
has changed accordingly.[36]

In the same way, the figure of The Elephant Man has overtaken the real Joseph Merrick. And his unaccountable face
still issues forth a continual flow of artistic catachreses—
monstrously mixed metaphors.

FACE CRAFT

When The Elephant Man appeared in Michael Jackson's 1989 video for "Leave Me Alone," he was depicted as an elephant skull atop a human skeleton. This is less a cartoon and more of a hybrid visual pun, an animetaphor. The two dancing figures exhibit the features of racial "animatedness" Sianne Ngai describes in her book *Ugly Feelings*. Analyzing stop-motion animation, Ngai argues that the "seemingly neutral state of 'being moved'" has been "twisted into the image of the overemotional racialized subject, abetting his or her construction as unusually receptive to external control."[37] This music video is also an early version of the racialized logic of the internet meme, which Aria Dean describes as "dematerialized," "depersonalized," "in circulation," "atomized and multiplicitous," but also "vulnerable to appropriation and capture."[38] Both Ngai and Dean argue that the animation of non-white people seems to usurp their agency—they become automatons, puppets, splices of energetic life disconnected from human subjecthood, unable to "stand on their own." But both critics also note that animatedness offers the possibility for spontaneous, unexpected agency, an "unaccounted-for autonomy."[39]

When we admire Jackson's virtuosic dance movements, we are praising this ambivalent animatedness. But we can catch traces of this ambiguous agency in his face as well—and that helps us understand the radical potential of the face as a form of craft, as a work of art. Rumored to have bought Merrick's skeleton, Jackson was obsessed with Cleopatra, too—he owned a painting of her death and staged a love affair with Egypt in his video for "Remember the Time." Jackson collected eccentricity like it was a hobby, but it seems fitting that he was rumored to be fond of the most famously beautiful face in history and the most famously distorted one.

Jackson himself wore a stranger and stranger face over time. He was diagnosed with vitiligo, a condition that causes the loss of skin color in spreading patches, but the public long assumed that he was bleaching his skin out of racial self-hatred. Jackson epitomizes the dread and the fascination we have about *playing* with the face, about remolding it into a work of art: the distortion of race, gender, sexuality, and ability it entails, the compulsive aesthetic labor of it. We often use the concept of the fetish to describe Jackson's motivations: he "fetishized" whiteness, or a childish idea of it—a thin nose and pale skin—that may have coincided with his sexual preferences.

But the other context in which Freud introduces the fetish—mourning—is fitting for Jackson's face too:

In the analysis of two young men I learned that each—one when he was two years old and the other when he was ten—had failed to take cognizance of the death of his beloved father—had 'scotomized' [mentally blocked] it—and yet neither of them had developed a psychosis

. . . But further research led to another solution of the contradiction . . . It was only one current in their mental life that had not recognized their father's death; there was another current which took full account of that fact. The attitude which fitted in with the wish and the attitude which fitted in with reality existed side by side.[40]

Walter Benjamin argues that the cult value of art—what he calls its "aura"—doesn't disappear with the advent of photography: "It retires into an ultimate retrenchment: the human countenance . . . The cult of remembrance of loved ones, absent or dead, offers a last refuge for the cult value of the pictures. For the last time the aura emanates from the early photographs in the fleeting expression of a human face. This is what constitutes their melancholy, incomparable beauty."[41] As with Freud's patients who both believe and don't believe in their fathers' deaths, the picture of a face both shines with the aura of presence and with the sense that it is fleeting, that the face belongs to a corpse. To look at *before* and *after* pictures of Jackson's face, even before his death, has always been to experience this sense of glowing grief.

It feels somehow wrong to say that our disavowal, the way we compensate for the loss of a person, is *pleasurable*. But it is certainly strange and unaccountably riveting to watch Jackson's blackness and vibrancy and fleshy plenitude dissolve as we turn from *before* to *after*, a decay before death, all the more poignant in that it may have been preventable. Our continued fascination with Jackson's will to deface, or un-face, himself is not a mourning ritual—which would have a sense of resolution, a peaceful letting go. It is, as Benjamin's language suggests, a *melancholy* attachment: we can't quite relinquish the glowing younger Michael. We bring it continually to the fore, juxtaposing it with that whitewashed older Michael. We look at them, back and forth, a fetishistic, masochistic oscillation.

Again, perhaps outrageously, I'm tempted to ask: what if we thought of Jackson's addiction to plastic surgery—which killed him, insofar as it made him addicted to the painkillers he overdosed on—not as self-loathing body modification, but as a form of artistic practice? This does not make it, nor him, more forgivable. But it shifts the lens through which we view his face. We no longer read it as a failure to attain The Ideal Face, nor as his psychological damage writ visible. Rather, it conjures that confounding admixture of pain and ambition, of suffering and double consciousness, that artists use as a crucible in which to forge a complex art. What can't be denied is that Michael Jackson, Joseph Merrick, and Cleopatra each made their strange faces a shameless spectacle. Doesn't this reject the notion that strangeness is a matter of shame at all?

2.

TWO-

FACED

AUTHENTICITY AND DUPLICITY

One day in the middle of the nineteenth century, a woman sat down to write. She dipped her goose quill in the iron gall ink—a purply, brownish black—that was popular until the 1860s. She wrote on embossed stationery, folded into folios and ruled with thin blue lines—a kind of paper distinctive to the library of the planter and slaveholder John W. Wheeler. Occasionally she would cross out a word or a phrase, and inscribe or paste its substitute in the space above or beside the strike-out. The story was sentimental and theatrical. The Gothic, the adventure tale, and the melodrama were woven together; stretched over the sturdy plot of a more recent genre, the slave narrative; then embroidered with allusions to the Bible, the ancients, and British writers like Byron, the Brontës, and Dickens. The woman titled her manuscript "*The Bondwoman's Narrative*, By Hannah Crafts, A Fugitive Slave Recently Escaped From North Carolina."[42]

It was bound in cloth and stored in an attic in New Jersey for nearly a century. An esteemed African-American librarian named Dorothy Porter Wesley bought it from a New York City bookseller in 1948 for $85 and added it to her monumental private collection. In 2001, it went up for auction at Swann Galleries, and Harvard Professor of African-American Studies Henry Louis Gates, Jr. bought it for $8500. Gates set about authenticating it, trying to establish both when it was published and by whom. Once he'd gathered data from book collectors and scholars, he published an article in *The New Yorker* announcing his discovery of the manuscript. If its author (like her titular heroine) had truly been enslaved, and if the story were truly written before the Civil War (which goes unmentioned in it), then this was a scholarly breakthrough: the only known novel written by a fugitive from slavery and the first by an African-American woman.

In his article, Gates finds it "a quirky novel" with a "snobbish" narrator, but takes pains to prove that it was autobiographical—that the details in the manuscript, "a record of plain unvarnished facts," according to its preface, were traces of its author. "She describes the winter in Washington with the vividness of someone who may have seen it for herself," Gates speculates,[43] then quotes her:

> Gloom everywhere. Gloom up the Potomac; where it rolls among meadows no longer green, and by splendid country seats. Gloom down the Potomac where it washes

the sides of huge war-ships. Gloom on the marshes, the fields, and the heights. Gloom settling steadily down over the sumptuous habitations of the rich, and creeping through the cellars of the poor. Gloom arresting the steps of chance-office seekers, and bewildering the heads of grave and reverend Senators; for with fog, and drizzle, and a sleety driving mist the night has come at least two hours before its time.[44]

This is virtuosic prose, rife with social commentary on a city that was—and still is—more shacks and mansions than rags-to-riches. But it is, of course, prose borrowed from Dickens: "Fog everywhere. Fog up the river, where it flows among green airs and meadows . . ." Neither Gates nor his *New Yorker* editors initially acknowledged the echoes of this passage from *Bleak House*. Gates did a Q&A in the next issue to explain Crafts's "borrowings—occasionally verbatim"—with his reassurance that her "copying wasn't mindless." Copying. Sampling. Riffing. Plagiarizing?

Crafts's manuscript was never published in her time, and copyright law didn't exist back then. But the discovery that her purported "slave narrative," already too riddled with unlikelihood to be a literal autobiography, had these near-exact imitations of British authors' prose posed a different kind of problem. Not a legal one, but a literary one: how can you authenticate someone who didn't just write "truth stranger than fiction" but someone else's truth? Is Crafts a *real*

African-American writer, given the scanty historical record of her origins? Is Crafts even a real *writer*, given that she "lifted" large chunks of text from white nineteenth-century novels?

When Gates published a complete edition of *The Bondwoman's Narrative* in 2002, it was immediately greeted with skepticism about Crafts's authorship and racial identity. Take John Bloom's snide review:

> Gates would have us believe that a woman in her twenties, escaping in 1857 from a slave state that forbids the education of blacks would complete a 301-page novel before 1861, and that this novel would show an intimate familiarity with, among other things, the conventions of sentimental novels, Gothic novels, "the law of the Medes and Persians," the "lip of Heraclitus," and words like "magnanimity," "obsequious," "vicissitudes," "hieroglyphical" and "diffidence."[45]

Notwithstanding Bloom's ignorance of the erudition of the formerly enslaved like Frederick Douglass and Phyllis Wheatley, the white reviewer's rhetoric is painfully similar to that of an 1839 reviewer of a memoir in *The Christian Examiner*: "We read, in what professes to be the language of a slave, that which we feel a slave could not have written."[46]

To counter anachronistic claims like Bloom's, critics like John Stauffer adamantly insist on Crafts's authenticity as an African American and as a writer:

Hannah Crafts was, until the publication of *The Bondwoman's Narrative*, an invisible woman. With no formal education, she became one of the most literate and literary African Americans of her day. She refuted southern laws and the beliefs of most whites that kept blacks from learning to read and write, devoured almost every book she could get her hands on, including many classics of her time, and wrote the first extant novel by an African American woman. It is a brilliant novel, intricately nuanced and extraordinarily sophisticated in its story telling technique.[47]

These two opposed contemporary opinions both take the existence of a black literate Hannah Crafts to be *incredible*— the difference is that Bloom is incredulous, Stauffer admiring.

In 2005, two British critics, Celeste-Marie Bernier and Judie Newman, wrote an article arguing that Hannah Crafts was neither a fugitive slave nor a black slave nor even an American slave. Their reading of the evidence suggests to them that Crafts was as likely to be white as black and that "the deep structure of the novel, the unconscious evidence of Hannah's real-life experience is that of a servant, not a slave, obsessed by her mistress, admiring of the great house, demarcating her territory as opposed to that of the slaves, and with absolutely no sense of real solidarity with them."[48] To be fair, there is more than one historical example of this kind of literary blackface, although Gates points out just how rare it was in Crafts's time.[49]

It's striking how often claims for Crafts's whiteness and claims for her blackness echo each other. So, where Gates cites Crafts's class snobbery as a sure sign of her blackness, Bernier and Newman say it proves her whiteness, confirming "Crafts's interests in distancing herself not only from black culture, but also from other black slaves, in ways which go further than slave narrators keen to express their exceptional status."[50] Gates finds it unlikely a white abolitionist would dare depict explicit stereotypes; Bernier and Newman find it "unlikely that during the abolitionist period any antislavery writer would concede as far as to expose black slaves unequivocally as 'brutalized specimens of humanity' bereft of any redeeming features."[51]

Why did the question of Crafts's race become an index of her literary legitimacy? As the debate about the true identity of William Shakespeare and, more recently, the one about that of the Italian author Elena Ferrante suggest, we seem to have an unquenchable desire to meet the author—to "put a face to the name," as they say, and, in the case of Crafts, a race to the face as well.

This desire is so strong that the compendium that Gates published in 2003, entitled *In Search of Hannah Crafts*, even included a portrait of one of his historical suspects, a woman named Jane Johnson. And when you Google "Hannah Crafts" now, an image of a woman crops up on the little Wikipedia window on the search page. Some hunting is required to learn that this is in fact Dorothy Porter Wesley, the librarian who first bought Crafts's manuscript, photographed by Carl Van Vechten in 1951. Both of these images are equally unlikely, historically speaking. They compensate for the woman we can't see, the writer whose face has vanished into history.

The debate over *The Bondwoman's Narrative* conflates several factors that fall under a larger opposition between *authenticity* and *duplicity*: Crafts's skin color, her history, her education, and her class (when enslaved and after). The roots of the word "authenticity" are the prefix *aut-*, which signifies selfsame, and *-hentes*, doer or being; combined, they yield "one who does a thing himself, a principal, a master, an autocrat." The word "duplicity" is from *duplex*, which breaks into *duo* two + *plic-* to fold; the word is itself double, meaning either "deceitfulness, double-dealing" or "the state or quality of being numerically or physically double or twofold: doubleness."[52] We have a very simple binary, perhaps the simplest of all: one versus two.

Since Plato, fictions have been denigrated as mimetic and manipulative, the two sides of duplicity. But what does it mean to be an authentic fiction writer? To tell the truth? To tell your own lie? Literary authorship seems to need authenticity and duplicity in equal measure. The word *craft* means either "skill, skillfulness, art; ability in planning or performing, ingenuity in constructing, dexterity" or "skill or art applied to deceive or overreach; deceit, guile, fraud, cunning." Does the name "Crafts" attached to *The Bondwoman's Narrative* suggest craftsmanship or craftiness? Is Hannah a canny palindrome, self-divided, self-reflective? And does her inclusion of what was likely her real name, *Bond*, in her title imply that her word is her bond or is it a sly allusion to bond paper?

Gates published *The Bondwoman's Narrative* with Crafts's edits intact—the text she struck out appears with a line through it like ~~this~~. This layered doubleness on the page is an uncannily apt textual figure for the story itself, its literary antecedents, and its belated reception. In the nineteenth century, slave narratives had to be authenticated by white figures of authority. Hence those strange frontispieces bearing two names, that of the black author and that of the white witness to its veracity, two people to signify the singularity (the originality and the single-person authorship) of one. Racial authenticity was enmeshed with literary authenticity in the slave narrative; it was key that the horrors of slavery be the truth of experience, rather than concocted as part of a political masquerade. But Crafts's "slave narrative" reads like a novel. Its improbable plot coincidences and exaggerated characters are foundational, not mere filigree.

Karen Sánchez-Eppler argues that the slipperiness of the text is neither fluke nor flaw, but rather a test of our own tendencies toward categorization:

> *The Bondwoman's Narrative* is an extremely hybrid work . . . This mixing of genres is not unique to this book; indeed such hybridity proves to be a quite general characteristic of African American writing in the 1850s. The questions of authenticity and genre that permeate the present publication of this manuscript—was she a slave? was she

black? is this a novel? is it true?—echo nineteenth century
concerns. Such questions arise . . . from a bed of essen-
tialist assumptions: that slaves are black, that freedom is
white, that novels falsify, that race and genre ought to be,
if ever they could be, pure. The power of Crafts's interpretive freedom derives from her persistent disruption of
all such axioms.[53]

In the manuscript, though, Crafts does not actually *disrupt*
the racial binary per se. Rather, she *manipulates* it, turns it
to strategic advantage. She doesn't destroy or even question
divisions of race—or fiction or class or gender—but rather
maintains them as manifest phenomena that her heroine can
exploit to her benefit. Rather than portraying Hannah and
the text as hybrid, as blended or mixed, she asks us to see
them as doubled, as twofold or two-faced. This is not a Janus
head looking in opposite directions, but a shifty layering of
surfaces—face and expression, physiognomy and countenance, darkness and light, black and white, truth and lie.

WHITE LIES

I first read *The Bondwoman's Narrative* in 2002, in a graduate
course on African-American literature taught by none other
than Professor Henry Louis Gates, Jr. In college, I'd studied
the famous Harlem Renaissance novels about "passing," James

Weldon Johnson's *Autobiography of an Ex-Colored Man* and Nella Larsen's *Passing*. Professor Gates's course introduced me to the longer history of the form, including works by Charles W. Chestnutt and William Wells Brown. Professor Gates once told us a story about the African-American minstrel performers, Bert Williams and George Walker: in taking a bow, one would raise his hat to flash a light-skinned wrist; the other would pull his hat off and bend at the waist to show off his wavy hair. Professor Gates teased me mercilessly for referring to this in class as "good hair," a term my mixed-race family had always casually bandied about. He was right. To conflate the unjustified privilege of a certain shade of skin or a certain texture of hair with a word like "good," which connotes inner virtue, isn't just unthinking; it's racist.

This confusion of surface and depth is in fact key to *The Bondwoman's Narrative*, especially given the kerfuffle around its publication—which Professor Gates admitted to us, insofar as he actively encouraged us to seek out and write about other texts that Crafts's novel was alluding to or riffing on. I remember there being a fevered sense of freedom in reading this newly discovered book. We didn't yet know who Crafts was; any desire to capture her intention, to put a face to the name, was suspended. All we had were the facing pages of the text, riven here and there with those beguiling, almost illicit struck-out lines.

The Bondwoman's Narrative recounts Hannah Crafts's life under slavery and her repeated, eventually successful, attempts to escape to freedom. This is complicated by her phenotype:

I soon learned what a curse was attached to my race, soon learned that the African blood in my veins would forever exclude me from the higher walks of life. That toil unremitted unpaid toil must be my lot and portion, without even the hope or expectation of any thing better. This seemed the harder to be borne, because my complexion was almost white, and the obnoxious descent could not be readily traced, though it gave a rotundity to my person, a wave and curl to my hair, and perhaps led me to fancy pictorial illustrations and flaming colors.[54]

She is "almost white"; her "African blood" tinges her person, hair, and personality; she is what we still call "light enough to pass." On one hand, Hannah is "black" only if we apply the one-drop rule, a biological, political, and social fabrication of the nineteenth century that nevertheless powerfully distorted the lived reality of the enslaved.[55] On the other hand, we dismiss her own claim to African descent and enslaved status only by ignoring the subtleties of her narrative.

In the racial logic with which we are still familiar in the United States, there's an external binary between black skin and white skin that would divide the enslaved Hannah from her white enslavers. But because Hannah's complexion is light, this gets reformulated as an internal binary. The inside and the outside of Hannah's body do not correspond. This maps onto a paradigm of language in which word and meaning are divorced.[56] Blackness is in her veins, but so removed from her visible skin that no one would identify her as "one of that miserable class" on sight.[57]

Hannah claims that the "lot and portion" of slavery is therefore that much heavier for her: not only does her biracial identity highlight the arbitrariness and injustice of that peculiar institution, but she alone must bear responsibility for it. That is, she feels obliged to tell the truth about her heritage. Her racial ambiguity poses an ethical dilemma as well as an existential one. If the myth of The Ideal Face posits it as the seat of truth—as the legible source of a person's true identity and intention—then *The Bondwoman's Narrative* works through a conundrum: what if your face lies?

Hannah tends to direct her "quiet way of observing things" toward "faces and characters." In her narrative, to be human is to have a face. When two women are discovered after spending several months in an abandoned cabin, they are barely recognizable: "Had we indeed lost all resemblance to human beings. We were crouched in the corner beneath our cloaks, and our head the only parts of persons visible, were disfigured by matted masses of hair, which feel [fell] over and vailed [sic] our faces." To participate in social life is to see other faces. The worst part of imprisonment is that "during all this time we saw not a human face with the exception of that old man's." To be sane requires faces, too: "[f]or two long weary years she only beheld one human face, and that one the jailer[']s. Then, wherefore wonder that her mind failed?"[58]

This all accords with the tradition of elevating The Ideal Face as *the* key to humanity. Yet Crafts undoes this figure by distinguishing between the face and the "countenance":

> He had a prominent nose, high cheek bones, and black ugly teeth slightly protruding from his mouth at all times, . . . having the most disagr[e]eable appearance . . . But it was the expression of his countenance after all that made me shrink from and fear him. It was so dark, so sinister and sneering. It told so much of malice, of hate, of dislike to the beautiful the good and true.[59]

The phrenological impulse to read the bones of the face meets a psychological impulse to read its expression. These processes presuppose a kind of simultaneity of two faces: the literal, fixed features and the more expressive, flexible countenance. Here, they say the same thing. But the very separation of the face into two layers suggests that surface and depth don't necessarily match.

This double vision of the face emerges in a remarkable passage when Hannah peruses the family portraits at Lindendale, the plantation where she lives and works:

> Memories of the dead give at any time a haunting air to a silent room. How much more this becomes the case when standing face to face with their pictured resemblances and looking into the stony eyes motionless and

void of expression as those of an exhumed corpse. But even as I gazed the golden light of sunset penetrating through the open windows in an oblique direction set each rigid feature in a glow. Movements like those of life came over the line of stolid faces as the shadows of a linden played there.[60]

Light and shadow grant not just animation to the "pictured resemblances," but expression, dimension, and solidity, too. Elaine Scarry describes this operation of literary instruction as the "glide of the transparent over the surface of something underneath," which wipes out then restores that solid underlying thing, conjuring depth and durability.[61] The stirring of the portraits' stony, void eyes to life—to movement, to dimension—is reversed when an enslaved woman is gibbeted from the same linden tree: "her rigid features assumed a collapsed and corpse-like hue and appearance, her eyes seemed starting from their sockets, and her protruding tongue refused to articulate a sound."[62] To live is to have a face—or rather two faces, the physical form always haunted by the possibility of expression, be it in the eyes, the mouth, or the countenance.

Hannah's biracial face paints a white portrait, her blackness *just* visible like a sepia overlay. And what of her *bifacial* face? When she is sold to a new owner, he says, "I believe that Hannah can be trusted. I almost know she can. I see it in her countenance, and I've got eyes that ~~most ofte~~ are seldom deceived in the human face." But as the novel proceeds, we find that Hannah, despite all her Bible-thumping about honesty, has learned from her masters the art of polite dissemblance, of "coaxing and flattery." As Hannah depicts it, the code of conduct within slave plantation culture is at best one of indirectness and persuasion, at worst, one of outright deception and duplicity. So, when Hannah serves at a dinner, she observes "youthful faces and faces of two score that strove to cheat time, and refuse to be old . . . a glare and glitter [of] deceitful smiles and hollow hearts." Her later description of the scene in Washington, DC, the one which riffs heavily on Dickens's evocation of Chancery Court in *Bleak House*, is a parody of patronage and lobbying: "all who had offices to bestow had been coaxed, and flattered, and addled by female tongues untill they scarcely knew what they were about."[63]

We rarely find Hannah herself telling an outright lie, however. Indeed, much is made of her decision *not* to lie to strangers whom she encounters after she escapes from slavery. Hannah finds herself in a strange bind—her rescuers are white but do not recognize her as black. At first, when she is asked the name of her master, Hannah tells the truth, "[n]ot perceiving that any good could come of concealment." When she realizes that a rescuer thinks she's white, she wonders: "Should I perpetuate the delusion, or acknowledge frankly my humble condition. I was sorely tempted, but only for a moment. My better nature prevailed."[64] This combination of pragmatism and moral reasoning for her truth-telling leads her, naturally, to utter what we call white lies.

Consider how her logic proceeds when she makes her first duplicitous decision not to disclose the racial "truth" about herself and her mistress:

> We could not be utterly forsaken, and hopeless and help-less when God was near. We had committed no crime and what had we to fear? We had not the appearance of fugitives from slavery. No one there could recognize who and what we were. We could easily reach the house I had discovered, where perhaps we could ascertain all we desired to know.
>
> This plan I communicated to my mistress. At first she hesitated, declaring that detection would be worse than death.
>
> "But there can be [no] detection" I replied.
>
> "Oh: I don't know I don't know" she answered wringing her hands.
>
> "I can see no reason why we should fear it. We will represent ourselves as poor women who have become accidental[l]y lost."
>
> "Which will be no more than the truth" she said with a sudden energy.
>
> "Certainly it will be the truth, and as such we will tell it. Now let us go."[65]

Hannah shifts so rapidly from extolling their faith and inno-cence to weighing their chances of detection that it almost goes unnoticed that the plan here is to pass as white. Hannah's mistress—who also, as it turns out, has the "obnoxious descent" of blackness—extenuates this white lie by fervently insisting that it "will be no more than the truth." Hannah concurs, in the future tense—"it will be the truth." Words are contextual. Not only are these words true now if we omit the frame of slavery that would deny these women even the dignity of poverty, but they also *will become* true in some future when the distortions of race have ended. Hannah's ability to turn language to duplicitous purposes thus relies on a biracial and bifacial split in identity as well as a split in time.

BLACKENED REPUTATIONS

Hannah's most duplicitous act involves both the word and the flesh. It takes place at the very center of coaxing and flattery: the elite circles of Washington, DC. And it is an act of revenge against her mistress, Mrs Wheeler, who signifies the apex of hypocrisy in the text. Mrs Wheeler has a "bland, soft, insinuating" voice and a "languid air" that can be "dropped for a moment, then taken up and put on again, as though it were a mantle."[66] Mrs Wheeler reveals the depth of her duplicity in the very process of procuring Hannah:

> That afternoon she dictated a letter for me to write. It was to my prospective master, and the subject was myself. It opened as business letters usually do, very brief and concise. Then it

stated that she, (Mrs Wheeler) was visiting Mrs Henry, that she had seen me, that I was very homely, and what was worse a bigot in religion; that I wept and shuddered at the idea of being transferred to his family, though I was very fond of her, and that my earnest solicitations had induced her to offer to purchase me, though she could not give anything like a great price, as she had many doubts of my ability to serve her properly, and thought from my previous character that I would be likely to run away the first opportunity.

No one can doubt that I hesitated to pen such a libel on myself.[67]

Mrs Wheeler shames Hannah for objecting to this portrait— "Do you wish me to write that you are very beautiful and good?"—and adds insult to injury by telling the "open and guileless" Mrs Henry that Hannah is "perfectly satisfied with the contents" of this "beautiful letter."[68]

Hannah is forced into a strange complicity with Mrs Wheeler's predictable and empty cruelty. If Hannah wants to hold onto her self-perception as humble, kind, and pragmatic, then she must assent to the fabrication, which Mrs Wheeler claims is in Hannah's best interests: "All in the way of a bargain, my dear."[69] And if Hannah hesitates in the writing of this letter, it does not change anything: at the end of the scene, the letter is simply sealed and sent, suggesting that Hannah inscribes the dictated contents before she makes her discomfort about them known.

But words are contextual, as Mrs Wheeler cynically points out: "I think you quite beautiful but of course others might not; then you are doubtless very good, yet some might consider your notions of religion and truth as highly improper for one in your station, and of course you prefer the service of a lady to that of a gentleman." Hannah may not like this picture of herself; that doesn't mean it's not true. For how can one truly *know* oneself? Besides, when you're surrounded by the distorting mirrors of poverty, slavery, racism, and sexism, what is truth anyway?[70] Well, the narrative tells us, truth is a question of power:

> I never felt so poor, so weak, so utterly subjected to the authority of another, as when that woman with her soft voice and suavity of manner, yet withal so stern and inflexible told me that I was hers body and soul, and that she did and would exact obedience in all cases and under all circumstances. "And yet" I thought "Mrs Henry told me how kind you were."
>
> But the best and wisest may be deceived.
>
> ~~service This I readily engaged to do, wishing not only to oblige the lady, but to show my gratitude to Mrs Henry The next morning I was duly installed~~.[71]

This is a crucial moment in Hannah's transition from a passive two-facedness toward a strategic one. Crafts cuts two lines describing Hannah's usual acquiescent kowtowing, and gives us instead a rhetorical flourish, a crisp cliché that looks both forward and backward. While "the best and wisest may be deceived" seems simply to lament Mrs Henry's gullibility, in retrospect, we see that it also foreshadows the deception of the (supposed) "best and wisest" in the scene ahead.

Preparing to make a good impression on some high society folks, Mrs Wheeler asks Hannah to help her procure and apply a popular new powder for whitening the skin. Unusually, Hannah flatters her mistress: "I had never seen her look better." Mrs Wheeler almost forgets her smelling bottle, which Hannah passes to Mr Wheeler to hand to his wife in her carriage. When Mrs Wheeler returns from her errand, the household is in for a shock, "for though the vail [sic], the bonnet, and the dress were those of that lady, or exactly similar, the face was black."[72] Only then does Hannah reveal (to us, too) that she actually knew this might happen when she gave the powder and the smelling bottle to Mrs Wheeler. That is, she wears a poker face even as she dramatizes the absurd visual logic of finding race in the face:

> "The powder certainly is white, and yet it may possess such chemical properties as occasion blackness. Indeed I recently saw in the newspapers some accounts of a chemist who having been jilted by a lady very liberal in the application of powder to her face had invented as a method of revenge a certain kind of smelling bottles, of which the fumes would suddenly blacken the whitest skin

provided the said cosmetic had been previously applied."

"You wretch" exclaimed the lady suddenly opening her eyes. "Why didn't you tell me of this before?"

"I—I—didn't think of it, didn't know it was necessary" I stammered in extenuation.[73]

Hannah's actions, on paper, are clean: she followed orders and kept mum. But Mrs Wheeler is right to suspect her. She has a clear motive: what better way to wreak revenge on her mistress—who forced her to blacken her own reputation in that libelous letter—than to make Mrs Wheeler suffer the injustice of being misread? What could be more apt than to blacken the face of a woman trying to be whiter? If the truth of race is a question of power, Hannah makes it a question of powder.

Crafts delights over the irony of the scandal: "Some viewed it in the light of a little masquerade; and thus taken it became extremely funny. Others considered it to have originated in a wager, and thought the lady rather debased herself. Very few regarded it as it really was, the deserved punishment of an act of vanity." Is there a knowing smirk behind Hannah's "I had never seen her look better"? Is there a little pride when she says, "Mrs Wheeler's notoriety extended to her husband, and even to me"? Hannah says Mrs Wheeler's later "allusion to that ludicrous circumstance actually forced me to smile."[74]

Again, Hannah doesn't lie, exactly. Rather, she withholds the truth, then gratuitously confesses it. This suits the crime she is punishing: in the letter, Mrs Wheeler made Hannah postpone the revelation of her true character until after her purchase. The difference between honesty and dishonesty is time; Hannah, too, manipulates time, rather than information, to her advantage. Her crafty use of silence allows her to present an innocent face (to her mistress; to the reader) while negotiating within a system built on duplicity, on coaxing and flattery.

Mrs Wheeler accuses Hannah of being not cannily, but *essentially* two-faced: "With all your pretty airs and your white face, you are nothing but a slave after all, and no better than the blackest wench." Hannah uses the same rhetoric about Mrs Wheeler's new handmaid Maria, "a dark mulatto, very quick motioned with black snaky eyes . . . an adept in the art of dissembling." When Maria frames Hannah, makes her "victim of a conspiracy," Crafts implies that this duplicity is visible in her face: "her countenance would be the smoothest and her words the fairest when she contemplated the greatest injury." And when Hannah is sent off to live among the field slaves, she claims she has been "accused of a crime of which I was innocent, my reputation with my Mistress blackened, and most horrible of all, doomed to association with the vile, foul, filthy inhabitants of the huts."[75]

Blackened skin, blackened motives, and blackened reputations are all lumped together here. But this slippage comes to seem more of a pun on "black" than a real causal trajectory. This is in part because Crafts makes each type of blackening highly contingent, again on context and time. We come to see biological, social, and moral "blackness" as surface phenomena. They can all be conjured at will, undone in a moment, or enforced simply by placing someone in a new setting. When Mrs Wheeler makes Hannah marry and live with a dark-skinned "field slave," she tries to consign Hannah to an inflexible racial position. This "blackening," not of Hannah's skin, but of her reputation, her situation, and implicitly, her posterity, seems to preclude the possibility of passing out of the space of the plantation, or even of maneuvering within its intricate codes.

But this just forces Hannah to become more strategic. She goes from withholding the truth about her body to actively disguising it. She assumes the double persona of a white man, donning "a suit of male apparel exactly corresponding to [her] size and figure."[76] She no longer hesitates about whether to reveal herself. No heavy-handed rationale for her lies here:

Occasionally I found friends, and this my disguise greatly facilitated. The people had no idea of my being a fugitive slave, and they were generally kind and hospitable.

I told them I was an orphan who had been left in destitute circumstances, and that I was endeavoring to make my way on foot to join the relatives of my mother who lived at the North. This account, so true and simple, greatly won the sympathies of all especially the women.[77]

Hannah has never met her mother and knows nothing of her relatives, but the narrative doesn't even flinch from the notion that this account is "true and simple." Hannah becomes a figure with so many faces, it becomes almost futile to seek just one. The world sees a white man; another runaway sees her as a black "brother"; we see our pale narrator, tinged with "African blood."

Eventually, Hannah encounters yet another version of herself, a bond-paper-woman:

> One day I stopped at a house and asked for dinner. It was generously bestowed, and during my repast the mistress of the mansion, a plain well-spoken woman, inquired if I had met a woman in my wanderings answering that description, and she held up a paper on which was delineated my exact size and figure, in female apparel. I commanded my countenance and voice sufficiently to answer in a natural manner that I had not.[78]

It seems like Hannah tells a lie. But in fact her reply (like her countenance, voice, and "natural" manner) is two-faced, both truth and lie. Figuratively, she does not recognize this version of herself, because she does not feel it to be true. But literally, too, the truth of the matter is that she has not actually "met" the woman on the page. For how can one truly *meet oneself*?

Crafts's two-faced language puts us in the place of the enslaved, who were subject to the duplicity of language every day. This is perhaps why she doesn't shy from the other two-facedness of which her narrative has been accused: her "borrowings." Regardless of how mindless or knowing it was, Crafts's use of canonical masks is so patent, it can hardly be called plagiarism—it isn't *sneaky* enough. It does not hide or prevaricate. Rather, when she turns Dickens's fog to gloom, and eventually to mud, Crafts literally blackens it. This is what we call signifying, an African-American rhetorical practice that also goes under the names: *the dozens*, *reading*, *rapping*, and yes, *telling lies*. Kevin Young notes: "For the black author, and even the ex-slave narrator, creativity has often lain with the lie—forging an identity, 'making' one, but 'lying' about one too."[79] I myself was born to a black mother and a white father; my face is the color of milky tea; I've never been mistaken for white. I did, however, once bet someone they couldn't guess where I'm from. I won. If your face is already a lie, why not make it a story?

3.

MOP

HEAD

SUBSTITUTE

In one trailer for his 1960 film *Psycho*, Alfred Hitchcock gives us a tour of the Bates Motel and the American Gothic house behind it. With that gooey glum voice of his, he offers tidbits about the film as he strolls around, gradually making his way to the bathroom in Marion Crane's motel room—both the point and the end of the tour. Hitchcock steps inside and says:

> Well, they've cleaned all this up now. Big difference. You should have seen the blood. The whole, the whole place was . . . Well it's, it's too horrible to describe. Dreadful. And I tell you, there's a very important clue was found here. Down there [points at the toilet]. Well the murderer, you see, crept in here very slowly, of course the shower was on, there was no sound, and . . .

He pulls the shower curtain back to reveal a screaming woman, her face soon covered by the film's title, her shrieks soon drowned by the violin strokes of Bernard Herrmann's score. A funny factoid about this trailer: the face behind the curtain does not belong—as it does in the film—to Janet Leigh, who plays Marion Crane. It belongs to her co-star, Vera Miles, who plays Marion's sister Lila. Miles stepped in for the trailer because Leigh was sick. It's hard to tell, not just because of the title that serves as a handy fig leaf, but also because the two actresses looked so alike. Miles simply donned a wig for the part that day.

Hitchcock had to have been aware, when he cast the Crane sisters, that his two lead actresses were dead ringers for each other, so to speak. And if the similarity between the two women's faces "can be easily explained" by their family connection in the film, critic Robin Wood wonders:

What of that, still more striking, between Anthony Perkins [who plays Norman Bates] and John Gavin [who plays Sam Loomis]? As they face each other across the counter of Norman's office, we have the uncanny feeling that we are looking at two sides of the same coin . . . the two men look at each other, and we look at them, and we realize suddenly that they are interchangeable: each seems the reflection of the other (though a reflection in a distorting mirror), the one healthy, balanced, the other gnawed and rotted within by poisoned sex. Similarly, Vera

Miles is the extension of Janet Leigh, and what she sees
is, potentially, inside herself. The characters of *Psycho* are
one character, and that character, thanks to the identifi-
cations the film evokes, is us.[80]

Wood's conclusion offers a familiar understanding of Gothic
doubling: the external figure of the doppelgänger intimates
that corruption or monstrosity or perversion lurks within.

For instance, Hitchcock's cameo in *Psycho*—outside
Marion's office, capped with an ironic Stetson—seems like
a double of Cassidy, the cowboy-hat-wearing client from
whom Marion steals $40,000. This theft sparks the plot, so
we dwell on this scene. As her co-worker Caroline looks
on, Cassidy makes grotesquely sexual remarks to Marion:
"Tomorrow's the day! My sweet little girl . . . Not you, my
daughter! A baby, and tomorrow she stands up there and
gets her sweet self married away from me."[81] The dialogue
briefly doubles the two female workers, too, and if you take
the fact that Hitchcock's daughter plays Caroline and "mix
a little gossip with a Freudo-structuralist logic of 'substitutions,'" Raymond Durgnat writes witheringly, "this scene has
a secret theme: it's Hitchcock's Unconscious confession of
incest and paedophilia."[82]

But the proliferation of similar faces in *Psycho* makes it
too difficult to pin down the doubling to a mere theme like
ethical duplicity or psychosexual perversion. For one thing,
the film glibly wraps up the plot with moral certitude about

who is corrupt and who isn't. Degrees of sin remain clear, "a sort of scale of the abnormal," as Francois Truffaut put it: "First there is a scene of adultery, then a theft, then one crime followed by another, and finally, psychopathy. Each passage puts us on a higher note of the scale."[83] All of *Psycho's* doubling doesn't translate in the end into equal-opportunity corruption for everyone. And for another thing, *Psycho's* faces are not *exactly* alike. Consider this: what if Hitchcock had cast the same actress for the parts of Marion and Lila, who are never in fact on screen at the same time? After all, he cast the same actress to play (what seem to be) two different women in *Vertigo*. As it turns out, the inexact similarity of the Crane sisters—Lila is a thinner, faded version of Marion—is key to *Psycho's* uncanny effects. Norman's face, too, is smaller than Sam's; it is later likened to Marion's face, and eventually, creepily overlaid with his mother's.

Psycho's faces are more like *substitutes* than reflections. As when Miles subbed in for Leigh in the trailer, the doubling in the film seems connected to Hitchcock's *expediency*, the sense of formal and literal economy surrounding his productions. A perfect example lies in the production details of the infamous shower scene, which all involve canny substitutions as well. The sound of stabbing Marion's body? A knife into a cantaloupe. Her splattered blood? Bosco chocolate syrup. There's some debate about whether Leigh was actually naked in the sequence (some claim to have seen b-rolls with a nip-slip), but most shots are of a body double or a dummy.

We all know now (spoiler alert) that the silhouette behind the curtain isn't really Norman's mother. Nor, however, is it technically Norman. While in the plot, it's Norman in a wig, with a mother complex, the figure in the scene was played not by Anthony Perkins but by a female extra; in the murder of Detective Arbogast, Mother was played by yet another woman. Even Mother's voice splices the voices of two women and a man, sometimes within the same sentence.[84]

Along with these logistical substitutions—inexact but efficient, delightful to discover—the shower scene also revolves around filmic substitutions. The multiple cuts of the scene (at least 50) rely on a montage: the viewer sees a slashing knife, spurting blood, and a shrieking, cowering body, and makes some warranted assumptions. Hitchcock deviates from the Hollywood mantra of smoothly stitching these shots together but in an economical way: the cutting up of film is made to evoke the cutting up of a body.

FETISH

One name for this logic of substitution is *fetishism*. The fetish in Hitchcock is by now a belated, decayed subject: fur, taxidermy, knives, coy sexual innuendo. I'm less interested in fetishism as a psychosexual condition than as a kind of economy. The word "fetish" emerged in the context of a cultural confrontation of fifteenth century Italian, Portuguese, Dutch, and West African merchants. *Fetish* is traceable to *factitious*, as well as to the Portuguese *feitico*, charm or sorcery, possibly a proto-coin, a common currency of exchange. A fetish can be natural or artificial, fashioned or conjured, and can either resemble the lost object (a meaningful substitution based on similarity) or happen to be nearby (an arbitrary substitution based on proximity). In anthropology, psychoanalysis, and Marxism, a fetish means, broadly, an object that becomes valuable by standing in or making up for a loss or absence. In some cultures, we worship idols that stand in for an absent god. In childhood or in mourning, we grow attached to objects that substitute for the loss of (imagined) genitals or people. And in capitalism, commodities conceal the conditions of their production, but also the loss of our relationships to reality, and to others.[85]

If *Psycho*'s similar faces are more *substitutes* than reflections, then we might say that they operate according to the logic of the fetish. Film theory has long considered the cinematic face a fetish, a kind of radiant derivative on screen that both conceals and substitutes for a real person. Walter Benjamin blames the loss of aura, in part, on the advent of film, which "split the actor's work into a series of mountable episodes," "multiple fragments which are assembled under a new law" (montage). Benjamin suggests that "the cult of the movie star, fostered by the money of the film industry, preserves not the aura of the person but the 'spell of the personality,' the phony spell of a commodity."[86] This phony spell covers over the loss of the unique person—the stage actress, the human herself. Gilles Deleuze calls this ersatz glow of the starlet's face in close-up "the affection-image."[87] To put it simply, the image on screen to which we attach our affections obviously depicts a real person but that person isn't actually there. The filmic face is a fetish for a sense of human presence and material reality—it glows, it beckons, it lulls us into a spell, it makes us forget that the actor isn't in the room with us, that they might never be with us ever again.

We can see how The Ideal Face works as a fetish for personhood in the first half of *Psycho*, where Janet Leigh—who died in 2004—got to shine. We often see her face in close-up because Hitchcock used the crew and stage from his TV show, *Alfred Hitchcock Presents*. The camera moves between medium shots of her face, keeping Marion securely in the position of our heroine. We see what she sees, and we see how her face registers what she sees. Her intentions are unspoken but her face seems to express them.

She briefly seems to come undone when she makes her getaway with the money. A Babel-like voiceover of the voices of her boss, client, sister, and co-worker discussing her theft accompanies a frame of her face as she drives. Lights and shadows spin across her cheeks and temple. But we can still correlate her expressions with her thoughts: Marion's face flinches with fear, pinches worriedly, subtly smirks. These are meaningful, legible expressions, all the more so contrasted with the fixed face of the highway patrolman (the Law) who wakes her up in her car, his sunglasses making him seem like a robot or an insect. Once she reaches the "safe haven" of the Bates Motel, Marion's face again traces a dramatic arc from worry about the theft to a resolve to correct it. This reaches its apex in the rapturous look on her face as she cleanses herself of the day's grime, and of her sins, in the shower.

With her murder comes the shattering of this iconic illusion of character depth. In the shower, terror interrupts the naked skin of her face, stretching it as she flings her head back and forth. The objects surrounding her come to resemble her, as if reminding us that she is becoming inanimate. The "porcelain" skin of the Hollywood star is placed next to literal porcelain; her finery becomes a plastic curtain ripped from rattling hooks; her hair, a dragging mop. The showerhead, seen from below, looks like a circle surrounded by twisting rays; this echoes her splayed hand, the draining water, and her dead eye, into which the camera twirls in a complex zoom before it pans out to reveal her cheek crumpled against the floor like a pair of panties.

A mosaic of formal substitutions, the shower scene is often said to prompt a substitution in the object of our affections as well. It came as a great surprise to *Psycho*'s original audiences that the movie star billed as the headliner to the film was murdered halfway through. A typical quote from *Psycho: The First Time*, a compendium of audience responses, reads: "We were really in shock from that, I mean, there was absolute silence in the rest of the film, people were in total mourning for the loss."[88] The loss of our seemingly living, breathing heroine produces a longing that seems almost to animate the camera in her stead. It peers into her dead eye and finds nothing. It pans back, forlornly scans the room, pauses on the newspaper-wrapped cash she has left on the table, then lifts to the window. Viewers, bereft of the heroine to whose very thoughts they have been made privy, cling to the next figure they see through its frame: Norman, who at this point seems entirely innocent, shouts over his shoulder at Mother about "blood," then runs down to the motel and into our arms. Heroine is swapped for hero.

In his 1962 conversation with Hitchcock, Truffaut suggested one reason this transition feels so smooth: "It isn't necessarily identification, but the viewer becomes *attached to* Perkins because of the care with which he wipes away all the traces . . . It's tantamount to admiring someone for a job well done." Hitchcock pointed instead to the moment Norman pushes Marion's car-cum-hearse into the swamp: "When Perkins is looking at the car sinking in the pond, even though he's burying a body, when the car stops sinking for a moment, the public is thinking, 'I hope it goes all the way down!'"[89] Just then, Norman pauses eating candy corn—a detail Perkins introduced and which beautifully links him to the snack-chomping audience—and waits with bated breath. When the car sinks, we exhale with relief and *with Norman*. He is, in essence, our fetish—the face to which we cling following the devastating loss of Marion.

But after this swamp scene, our emotional connection to Norman is broken once again, as the film shifts abruptly to two other characters, Lila and Sam. Except that their faces seem so . . . *familiar*. The appearance of these two lookalikes soon after the film implodes allows a kind of visual comfort, almost a do-over, that helps us get past the plot rift of the horrific, unexpected murder. All of the characters we next encounter attract our sympathy for different reasons, suggesting that they each temporarily stand in for the centrally framed, iconic face that dominated the first half of the film.[90] Our intense attachment to that face gives way to an attenuated attachment to several random faces, none of which is an exact or final substitute. We might say that the camera's pan across the motel room that nudged our gaze from Marion to Norman sets in motion a continual movement from face to face, or rather from entity to entity, for the rest of the film. It's not that Norman and Lila and Sam and Arbogast *are* Marion—nor are they just as lost and as bad, as in love and in trouble. The moral of *Psycho*'s doubled faces isn't that "we are all evil," but rather that we ought not view the face as the seat of good or of evil at all.

The transition from The Ideal Face to several faces shatters the premise and promise of a psychological or spiritual redemption. When our heroine dies, we are left with a stuttering series of faces and things that circulate in a system of exchange, a circus of pleasure rather than a hero's journey. Norman's labile face often collapses into an inscrutable blankness: expression comes to seem a manipulable over-lay rather than a revelation of the self. The camera cranes awkwardly beneath his jaw when he leans over the desk to look at the guest log. It fixates on and implausibly tracks Arbogast's terrified face as he tumbles backward down the stairs. The face's surface (the skin, expression) and depth (the soul, meaning) ripple apart—or rather they both become literal, the thin material stretched over the solid mass of bone atop our spines.

In this sense, *Psycho* teases us with the idea of the smooth-ly sculpted, familiar, legible starlet's face, only to distort, then destroy, then continually displace it. Once the star is dead, *Psycho* no longer requires our attachment to one character over another. *Psycho* does not care which face we see, or even whether it's human. The film thus turns us away from an ideal, intentionalist reading (taking the face as a figure for something meaningful) toward a pleasurable, diverting one (the face as a figure for another figure and yet another). The Ideal Face loses its privileged status as the ultimate fetish. It becomes just one of many things—fetishes—that stir inces-sant, unquenchable desire in *Psycho*.

This is what Hitchcock meant when he said, of *Psycho*, "It wasn't a message that stirred the audiences, nor was it a great performance or their enjoyment of the novel. They were aroused by pure film."[91] What if we *played with* rather than *attached to* people in a film? What does it mean to treat faces as pleasurable objects rather than seats of the soul? Is this callous or perverse? Does it debase the human? Or does it level the human with all of the other material entities around us?

MOP

Once The Ideal Face collapses into a set of fetishes, the face-as-thing and the thing-as-face exist on the same plane, each available for momentary interpretive fondling. This explains why so many objects in *Psycho* seem to have faces, from the many cars with their headlights for eyes, to the Gothic mansion itself. Hitchcock's take on Norman's taxidermical pets explicitly connects them to the gaze: "Owls belong to the night world; they are watchers, and this appeals to [Anthony] Perkins's masochism. He knows the birds and he knows that they're watching him all the time. He can see his own guilt reflected in their knowing eyes."[78] Guilt is the source of pleasure ("masochism") here, like the pleasure of wordplay around Norman's *hobby*: the word comes from the Old French, *hobet*, or falcon. The scene between Marion and Norman in the parlor is rife with avian double entendres that we might pick up only on second viewing: "[Mother's] as harmless as a stuffed bird"; "that expression, that one eats 'like a bird,' is really a fallac— I mean a falsity, because birds eat a tremendous lot"; "a hobby is supposed to pass the time, not fill it." Norman's taxidermy fills both dead bodies and dead time. These are all, of course, double fetishes—things that we take for persons, and images that we take for things.

The crowing fetish object in the film is Norman's mop. The word "mop" derives from the napkins used to wipe up the decks of merchant ships, invoking the anthropolgical origins of the fetish. A stick topped with a bush, it puts phallus ("fallac-") and fur—Freud's *ur*-images for fetishism—into contact. Its seeming autonomy on screen bespeaks Freud's interest in the uncanny, but also that spectral animation of the table in Marx's "Fetishism of Commodities":

> [T]he table continues to be that common, every-day thing, wood. But, so soon as it steps forth as a commodity, it is changed into something transcendent. It not only stands with its feet on the ground, but, in relation to all other commodities, it stands on its head, and evolves out of its wooden brain grotesque ideas, far more wonderful than 'table-turning' ever was.[92]

Durgnat describes the mop head in *Psycho* as "a creepy-crawly," "hair-spidery" thing; its bucket is "a black pit" in the film's phenomenology of the minor object, or the "sinister potential of *things*."[93] The recondite object stirs with life, performing "drastic" and "firework deletions."

The film also links the mop to Marion's corpse, that is, to loss.[94] Recall that whereas Truffaut ascribes our new attachment to Norman to his dexterous swinging of the mop in his clean-up act, Hitchcock suggests we become attached to

Norman because we share his relief at the sinking of the car. There is a moment that actually combines the two: when Norman is putting Marion's body and his cleaning tools into the trunk of her car, he accidentally drops the mop just as car headlights flash over him—another moment of bated breath that baits us into identifying with him. The mop imitates the body felled: it clatters to the ground, he tosses it in the trunk with the corpse, then buries both by sinking the car in the swamp. The mop seems to have served its fetishistic purpose, standing in for Marion's cleansing, purifying redemption, only to be buried.

But just as the dead Marion soon reappears for the viewer in the spectral form of Lila, Norman's mop, too, seems to resurrect later in the film:[95]

Lila is gazing up at the house above the Bates Motel, about to enter it, explore its recesses, and uncover the secrets haunting the film. The shot seems willfully incidental. It offers the backside of the motel to the viewer, the junk—etymologically from "old, inferior rope"—around Lila making a jumble of the film's investment in "waste." Curious Lila looking up at the house seems the ghostly reincarnation of her formerly curious, now deceased sister, a doubling reinforced by Lila's stark shadow. With this idea in mind, the scene's physical objects can't but invoke Marion's murder. Lila's long coat, pale in the sunlight, resembles the shower curtain that bisected life and death and in effect became Marion's shroud. The decrepit car with its ocular headlamps, backed by nature, gestures to Marion's twofold burial in the trunk and swamp.

And then there's the mop propped against the wall on the right, along with the bucket peeking out from the shadows at Lila's feet. Both recall Norman's meticulous clean-up of blood in the bathroom. On end, with its jaunty posture and spread hair, the mop seems to reach back even earlier than that bathroom cleansing scene, offering a lingering after-image of Marion's wetted hair dragging down white tile as she descended. The mop is like the animated broom in Disney's *Beauty and the Beast*, only creepier; it's where "be our guest" meets the vacancy sign.

Does this feel like I'm reaching? Reading too much into a prop—a piece of junk? When I first noticed it, I thought: *whoa!* Then: Wait, did I *see* that? I dug through

Psycho criticism to no avail, finding no mention of it even in Durgnat's frame-by-frame analysis, *A Long Hard Look* at *Psycho*. Nor does the mop reappear like this in Gus Van Sant's 1998 frame-by-frame color remake—given the oft-remarked bloodiness of his redo, maybe to leave it in the shot would beg too many questions. Because if you do notice it, it makes you wonder: Are we meant to recall that Norman put the original mop in the trunk? Or is this dramatic irony: clueless Lila standing beside a major clue to her sister's murder? Is this *The* Mop, come back to life? Or just *a* mop?

This whiff of the arbitrary is the crux of what the critic and theorist D.A. Miller calls Too Close Reading. Miller uncovers not one but three Hitchcock "cameos" in *Strangers on a Train*: the famous one of Hitchcock as a rotund passenger on the train (a person), and two previously unnoticed ones: the photograph of the director on the back of a book (a thing) and a barely visible shot of Hitchcock as a librarian (a shadow). One implication of this blatant latency—we might call it *blatency*—is that "the film might be hiding other objects, other 'Hitchcocks,' that are likewise visible but not apparent."[96] Like a detective or a reader of mysteries, "once you find a hidden picture, it seems always to have been there staring you in the face."[97] Miller explains how "the hidden picture, tampering with the readability of this emblem, making it a question or a problem, has such power to unsettle; with this neat little touch, Hitchcock's whole system seems momentarily to cloud over, to surrender its classic functionality to an enigmatic density."[98] Miller argues that this intimation of meaning draws the Too Close Reader "to details that, while undeniably intricate, are not noticeably important—little particulars that, though demonstrably meant, never strike us as deeply meaningful."[99]

This mop in *Psycho*—let's call it "the second mop"—sits just like this, on the cusp between the random and the meaningful. "Hidden in plain view," it invites interpretation but has somehow remained invisible to it. It raises a single, loaded question to which Miller draws our attention: is it a *clue* or an *error*? Strictly speaking, the second mop is explicable in terms of production or plot—but it *feels* like an error. It nags. It's either Norman's mistake to leave it there, or Lila's not to notice it, or Hitchcock's to present a detail *too* telling, too laden with symbolism to be incidental. In a sense, the scene at the back of the hotel is a snapshot of the slippage between fetishes that I've been describing. It is not meaningful so much as it is aesthetically pleasurable and intriguing. This shot offers three substitutes for the dead woman at the center of the film: it puts a shadow next to Lila next to a mop. In other words, like Hitchcock's three cameos in *Strangers on a Train*, it puts three versions of a *figure*—a shadow, a person, a thing—on a continuum of incidental fetishes.

SILHOUETTE

The things that Lila goes on to find in the house above the motel are all tinged with the human figure as well: a near-nude faux classical statue, a sculpture of hands in a Möbius clasp, Mother's loose hanging clothes, a bed imprinted with an S-curved form. Norman's room is chockablock with objects that bear the mark of childhood—like an old stuffed bunny that has been fondled frowzy—yet are juxtaposed with perverse pleasures: Lila opens a porn magazine and her eyes widen. Enacting fetishism's "baseless consecration of mundane material objects," Lila drifts from one quotidian thing to another, each in turn animated by her curiosity, which models our own.[100] And when she startles herself by catching her reflection in a mirror, her face comes to seem like just one among the many textured *things* she is encountering.

The film's ultimate fetish comes at the end of Lila's search: Mother. In deciding how to embody Norman's dead mother, Hitchcock replaced the script's "doll" with a wig-wearing skeletal corpse. When Lila spins Mother's chair, she sets the skeleton into motion, reminding us of the mop: the wooden look, the jerky movements, the thin layer of hair, the animation under a roving light. The corpse and the mop share a material shiftiness: heavy with water (or blood) yet light and stiff (as bone). Because we expect a murderer, a living person to whom we can pose questions, the skull seems oddly expressive and hollow at once: its open eyes and mouth imitate Lila's shocked expression—and ours—while still screaming DEATH.

This carried, handled, person-thing is how Norman compensates for the loss of Mother, but this fetish also covers over the dearth of a solution to the film's mystery. When Norman promptly barges in, dressed in a wig and a dress, swinging a knife at Lila, the terror—or camp—of the moment diverts us from a major plot inconsistency: how can Mother exist as both a corpse *and* as Norman in drag? Does he have two wigs? After two sister heroines, two male leads, two detectives, the two mothers in this scene constitute the illogical endpoint to the film's doubling.

And just as the buried mop seems to pop up again and again, Mother's skeleton re-emerges spectrally in the shot of Norman's face in custody:[101]

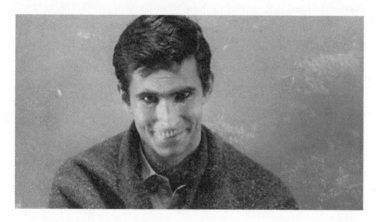

This layered flash-shot maintains and obscures both faces, resulting in an uneven materiality that maps onto the film's mishmash of psychobabble about Norman's mental imbalance. As the psychiatrist pontificates of Norman and his mother: "he began to think and speak for her, gave her half his life, so to speak. At times he could be both personalities, carry on conversations . . . at other times, the mother-half took over completely. He was never all Norman, but he was often only mother." As in Robert Louis Stevenson's *The Strange Case of Dr. Jekyll and Mr. Hyde*, the psyche does not divide easily into exactly two.[102]

The layered face in the penultimate shot of *Psycho* is no mere representation of Norman's alleged psychosexual schizophrenia, however—his "mummy" complex, so to speak. As Durgnat notes, a "lesser director might have had the death's head completely replace Norman's." Instead, as if pausing the film's endless drift from one face to another, Hitchcock creates a visual puzzle that, again, calls attention to the face as a *thing*. What is the *heft* of this doubled face? You might think it would be heavier than usual, but the image itself suggests the *lightness* of translucence. But even this kind of analysis threatens to break some law of humanity. *Psycho*'s sacrilege is gradually to objectify the face into a thing as palpable and graspable as a mop.

This counteracts not only the Hollywood face, but also The Ideal Face as the locus of ethics. Emmanuel Levinas's model of the face isn't literal but its physical and metaphysical attributes are far from incidental. He contrasts this ideal face to things, silhouettes, profiles, and money:

The face has no form added to it, but does not present

itself as the formless, as matter that lacks and calls for form. Things have a form, are seen *in* the light—silhouettes or profiles; the face signifies *itself*. As silhouette and profile a thing owes its nature to a perspective, remains relative to a point of view; a thing's situation thus constitutes its being. Strictly speaking a thing has no identity; convertible into another thing, it becomes money.[103]

Levinas's face that signifies itself looks a lot like the statuesque face that *Psycho* initially presents—in the form of Janet Leigh—only to reveal it to have always been a fetish, a mere surface that gave us the illusion of ethical relation. Once disillusioned, we can take pleasure in the flurry of facial fetishes that follow, even in the most horrific one—Mother's denuded face, stripped of skin, hollow at its core, yet campily delightful. This relation to the face does not deny, but delectates in its materiality, even its materialism, its seemingly infinite availability for circulation.

Alfred Hitchcock knew all about this. He made his own face into a profitable trope. His signature was a two-dimensional drawing in nine strokes:

The opening credits of *Alfred Hitchcock Presents*, the work that brought him the most money and fame, combines profile, caricature, and persona. The camera fades in on the line-drawing of his face. The white letters of the show's title overlay it, then disappear. Hitchcock's silhouette appears on the right and walks to center screen, eclipsing the caricature, which fades out. The silhouette shifts left and leaves us with a live three-dimensional Hitchcock intoning "Good evening, Ladies and Gentlemen."[104] In this sequence, Hitchcock undoes his own face, thins it out, layers it, makes it a surface, a gimmick to trope with, to joke with. His fetishism is less psychosexual than campy, his silhouette more like one of Goya's absurdist *caprichos* than staid portraiture.

Psycho, too, defaces the face, strips it of its privileged humanity, makes it as material, fungible, and pleasurable as the supreme fetish in Marx: money, printed profiles on paper cash or metal coins. One imagines a Hitchcockian currency bearing his silhouette, truly the anathema of The Ideal Face.

4.

BEAR

HEAD

THIS BLANK STARE

A lone, damp grizzly bear peruses lush vegetation at the top of a stream. Over the sound of the water, a heavy, gravelly voice intones:

> And what haunts me, is that in all the faces of all the bears that Treadwell ever filmed, I discover no kinship, no understanding, no mercy. I see only the overwhelming indifference of nature. To me, there is no such thing as a secret world of the bears. And this blank stare speaks only of a half-bored interest in food. But for Timothy Treadwell, this bear was a friend, a savior.[105]

The speaker is German director Werner Herzog. The man behind the camera is Timothy Treadwell, a self-appointed "eco-warrior" who spent thirteen summers recording his experiences living with (or perhaps just near) grizzly bears in the Katmai National Park and Preserve on the Alaskan

Peninsula. Herzog found over 100 hours of Treadwell's film reels in a producer's office and then edited, ordered, narrated, and spliced these fragments with his own footage to create the 2005 film, *Grizzly Man*.

Herzog conducted interviews with Treadwell's family and friends, and with the officials involved in the recovery, autopsy, and cremation of Treadwell's remains, which were found inside a 1000-pound bear with those of his girlfriend, Amie Huguenard. Herzog alludes to their mortal ends in this sequence: the phrase "half-bored interest in food" and the word "haunts" evoke the horrific breach of their bodily boundaries, and their passing to the other side. Herzog firmly divides himself from his main subjects by parodically aping Treadwell's language of affinity with the animals—"secret world of the bears," "a friend."

Herzog's language enacts what Marcus Bullock calls the two illusions of anthropomorphism. On one hand, "we pick something in our own human vocabulary of appearances to which we can see a correspondence, and then let that 'expression' speak to us as though we had made a reliable translation from one bodily form to another." The implication that there's something to see in the bear's face—that one *could* find kinship, understanding, mercy there—applies human psychology to the animal. Herzog's projection short-circuits in two near oxymorons: "half-bored interest in food" and "overwhelming indifference." On the other hand, we refuse "to see expressiveness," and "insist on hearing only silence and seeing only empty matter in the language of animal forms."[106] The bear's stare speaks but what it utters is "blankness." Jeremy Gilbert-Rolfe notes, "As the property of a face, [blankness] complicates communication, symbolically precluding communication by communicating incommunicativeness. The term 'blank expression' sums up the problem: It implies communication through noncommunication, the recognition of incomprehension."[107] In an anthropocentric catch-22, the bear's "blank" face both communicates ("speaks") and does not ("I discover . . . no understanding").

Herzog's anti-paean to the bear's "blank stare" thus reinscribes a set of boundaries that the marketing copy for *Grizzly Man* suspends ("In nature, there are boundaries. One man spent the last 13 years of his life crossing them"[108]), in particular what Herzog calls the "invisible line" between "humanness" and nature, across which the animal face stares at the human face. This is an old battleground, as one schism in nineteenth century scientific discourse suggests. Charles Bell's 1824 *The Anatomy and Philosophy of Expression* offers this famous aphorism on the subject: "expression is to passion what language is to thought." He draws a bright line between animals and humans, whose facial muscles he claims are divinely molded to express emotions. Darwin's 1872 *The Expression of the Emotions in Man and Animals* reformulates the paradigm by suggesting that "the force of language is much aided by the expressive movements of the face and body," and by seeking common ground—or shared heritage—for facial expression in both humans and animals. For Bell, we might say, the human face is a motivated and divinely authored sign; for Darwin, it is as contingent and worldly as natural selection.[109]

The debate continues into the twentieth century. Emmanuel Levinas argues: "The human face is completely different and only afterwards do we discover the face of an animal. I don't know if a snake has a face. I can't answer that question. A more specific analysis is needed."[110] An examination of Levinas's work shows that the luminous, naked, vulnerable face to which he returns is emphatically human, with perhaps one exception. He says that "the last Kantian in Nazi Germany," a dog named Bobby, lent dignity to the Jewish prisoners of war that he describes this way: "We were subhuman, a gang of apes." But even here, as Levinas's friend Jacques Derrida notes, we find a hierarchy of species ("subhuman") and a reduction of the most dignified animal to a mere witness: "this allegorical dog becomes . . . an other without alterity, without *logos*, without ethics, without the power to universalize maxims. It can witness to us only for us, being too other to be our brother or neighbor, not enough other to be the wholly other."[94]

In *The Animal that Therefore I Am*, Derrida contests this anthropocentric view. He notes that the question Jeremy Bentham posed about any living being in 1789—"can they suffer?"—undoes the animal/human binary, placing all creatures on the same side, with a shared relation to death:

"Mortality resides there, as the most radical means of thinking the finitude that we share with animals."[111] Like Darwin, Derrida levels the playing field of intelligence by speaking of "response" rather than "language": all creatures suffer; all creatures die; all creatures respond. Derrida also notes that the sheer diversity of animals makes an absurdity of "The Animal" as a conceptual category. Marx once put it as a kind of thought experiment: "It is as if, in addition to lions, tigers, hares, and all other really existing animals which together constitute the various families, species, subspecies, etc., of the animal kingdom, *the animal* would also exist, the individual incarnation of the entire animal kingdom."[112]

Finally, Derrida treats each animal as singular, its face a live surface, rather than merely an allegory or an idea: "the cat I am talking about is a real cat, truly, believe me, *a little cat*. It isn't the *figure* of a cat."[113] And this cat's face is active and perceptive. The animal "can allow itself to be looked at, no doubt, but also—something that philosophy perhaps forgets, perhaps being this calculated forgetting itself—it can look at me."[114] While the faces we've been examining so far in this book—on film, in texts—can easily reduce to objects or figures, Derrida and Herzog are both trying to describe what it feels like to encounter an animal face in real life. In that moment, the faces gazing across the "invisible line" at each other become two-sided; there is a surface and an interiority, an outside and an inside—on both sides. In this double interface, who is looking at whom?

Herzog seems to believe that the human directs the gaze and controls the distance. He films others who describe Treadwell's too-close relation to the animal world as contrived or dysfunctional. Interviewees accuse Treadwell of trying "to act like a bear" and report that he would "woof" at people he encountered in the wild; conversely, pilot Sam Egli says he treated bears as "people wearing bear-costumes." In Treadwell's footage, the animal face predominates: "Look at that face," he says to Timmy the fox, "Hey, thanks for being my friend." He even thanks the animals for his recovery from alcoholism: "I promised the bears that if I would look over them, would they please help me be a better person and they've become so inspirational, and living with the foxes too, that I did, I gave up the drinking. It was a miracle."

Treadwell perceives himself as both subject of and subject to the animals, as both fearless warrior and helpless vassal: "I will protect them. I will die for them, but I will not die at their claws and paws. I will fight. I will be strong. I'll be one of them. I will be . . . the master. But still a kind warrior." He flip-flops between self-abnegation—"I'm like a fly on the wall, observing, noncommittal, noninvasive"—and self-aggrandizement: "This is my land." When a bear that he dubs The Grinch gets too close, he punches her face, a terrifying breach of "safe distance," then professes love for her. This flirtation with human-animal contact ends in the ultimate communion of bodies. While he wanted to be face-to-face with animals, Herzog says, "Timothy came face-to-face with the harsh reality of nature."

Scholars and viewers often follow this logic, and perceive Treadwell's time with the bears as an escapist fantasy. One says he "christens the grizzlies with names that read like something from the pages of a strange book of mixed-up bedtime stories: Mr. Chocolate, Aunt Melissa, Demon Hatchet."[115] Others imply that only through his death does he truly "become animal": "it was not through his extraordinary sympathy with, knowledge, or imitation of bears, but through his frenetic squawking in the wilderness, and then, beyond language, through his death that he reached the threshold of the clandestine, the imperceptible, and . . . the molecular."[116] Treadwell "deconstructs the nature/culture binary" only because he was "enmeshed in the ecosystem," as susceptible to its "stresses and strains" as other animals, made vulnerable by "becoming prey," "becoming food," and "becoming meat."[117]

Herzog even includes a scene that portends Treadwell's "becoming shit." Treadwell picks Wendy the bear's dung off the ground: "It's warm. It just came from her butt. This was just inside of her . . . It's her life! It's her! And she's so precious to me. She gave me Downy," another bear. This double gift—the gift of Freud's anal stage and the gift of birth—gives way to the gift of death when a coroner, with wide eyes and wild gestures, later tells us that "inside this metal can was a plastic bag" containing Treadwell's bodily remains. A pilot laments, "we hauled away four garbage bags of people out of that bear."[118] At the heart of *Grizzly Man* lies this horror at the possibility that nature is "morally empty and indifferent towards human life." Herzog isn't afraid that the animal looks back. He's afraid that it doesn't: "this blank stare." The abyss between man and beast seems impassable, a chasm that will swallow us whole. And yet when you watch *Grizzly Man*, you find blankness everywhere—not just as a space of fear, but as a space of play, too.

THE BLANK SUBLIME

Herzog's work flirts with the natural world—"I like to direct landscapes just as I like to direct people and animals," he wryly comments—even as it often dwells on his sense of nature's overwhelming power.[119] This is a common mechanism in humans: we compensate for the incomprehensibility of nature by turning it into a source of pleasure. That mechanism goes by the name of the sublime. The sublime—etymologically "up to" (*sub-*) the "threshold" (*-limen*)[120]—operates across several boundaries: human/animal; man/nature; life/death; language/silence.

Grizzly Man continually rides these sublime lines: "Timothy lives at the frontier of this wilderness. He seeks it out, relentlessly, flirting with its dangers, playing with the idea of crossing over to the other side."[121] Willy Fulton, an Alaskan bush pilot, says Treadwell "definitely lived on the edge"; Treadwell describes himself as "edgy enough." He shirks the park regulation to "maintain at least 50 yards distance from the bears." In footage, his proximity to the bears is breathtakingly, "awfully close." He tells the camera, "there are times when my life is on the precipice of death," and later claims, "every second I move through this jungle or even at the tent, I am right on the precipice of bodily harm or even death."

Treadwell alludes here to two classic scenes of the sublime. One scene is the precipice—etymologically from "abrupt descent"—which suggests the steep cliff face, which still signifies the vastness and wonder of the natural world. As Schopenhauer notes, the "vault of the starry heaven" and "very high mountains" produce the feeling of the sublime through their "mere immensity in space and time." The other scene is the danger of death by tooth and claw, as Edmund Burke suggests: "There are many animals, who, though far from being large, are yet capable of raising ideas of the sublime, because they are considered as objects of terror."[122]

Treadwell is both always vulnerable to and claiming dominance over nature. Herzog recreates this tension by presenting aerial shots over the tangle of bush, as if visually enacting Treadwell's second-person self-address: "for the next two months or more you will be alone in this wild wilderness, this jungle that the bears have carved tunnels through. And that's the Grizzly Maze." Mapping the landscape as a "maze" "carved" by bears combines two forms of the sublime: an overwhelming natural phenomenon, one in which a man may, as Schopenhauer puts it, become "a vanishing nothing in the presence of stupendous might"; and a constructed complexity (a maze) that dazzles the mind to contemplate: "If we lose ourselves in the contemplation of the infinite greatness of the universe in space and time, meditate on the thousands of years that are past or to come, or if the heaven at night actually bring before our eyes innumerable worlds and so force upon our consciousness the immensity of the universe, we feel ourselves dwindle to nothing."[123]

Schopenhauer stresses the first term of Kant's definition of sublimity: a "*negative* pleasure."[124] Schopenhauer's example is not the stormy sea, but the empty plain: "a very lonely place, with unbroken horizon, under a cloudless sky, trees and plants in the perfectly motionless air, no animals, no men, no running water, the deepest silence . . . this is the species of the sublime for which the sight of the boundless prairies of the interior of North America is celebrated."[125] Wallace Stevens beautifully captures this American *blankness*:

Shall a man go barefoot?
Blinking and blank?
But how does one feel?

. . .

. . . the sublime comes down
To the spirit itself,
The spirit and space,

The empty spirit
In vacant space.[126]

Grizzly Man capitalizes on this "empty spirit" of the sublime, not just by evoking the empty landscape, but also by lingering over absence and infinity in both content and form.

Herzog's slow articulation of English maps onto his slow filmic takes: everything is dilated, and he often stretches out scenes in such a way that they leave or insert silence in the film. We watch Treadwell as he does several takes of "Wild Timmy Jungle Scenes" for a wildlife movie, each time sporting a different colored bandanna as he races down a path toward the fixed camera and begins a short monologue. When Treadwell shifts off frame, Herzog lets the footage roll without music, showing trees and brush wafting in the breeze. Herzog's voice-over eventually breaks the silence: "In his action movie mode, Treadwell probably did not realize that seemingly empty moments had a strange, secret beauty. Sometimes images themselves developed their own life, their own mysterious stardom." The absence of Treadwell here is all the more moving in contrast with his animated face in the previous scenes.

Perhaps the most important silence of the film is the scene in which Herzog himself appears on screen and listens to the tape from a handheld camera that was—by curse or luck—still running with the lens cap on during the bear's attack on Treadwell and Huguenard. His eyes closed, his head cradled in one hand, Herzog listens to the audio track through head-phones. He narrates some of what he hears but for the most part, the sequence is hidden from us. This twofold mystery creates a kind of giddy sublimity, a dizzying experience that depends on a dilation of sight and silence and seconds in the scene. This is intensified by a yawning *mise en abyme* of framing—we watch Herzog as he tries to picture what he hears. The many screens between us and death oddly do not distance us from it, but rather enact its utter incomprehensibility, deepening the "*negative* pleasure" of trying to see what we can't hear.

As if to emphasize this elision of the horror at the center of the film, there is a pseudo-witness present in this scene: Jewel Palovak, who describes herself as Treadwell's platonic friend but plays the part of a mourning widow in the film, and who has not yet heard the tape. Facing the director's lens, the handheld camera in her lap, Palovak stares intently, fingering an empty video case. Herzog, "after a long pause that prompts Palovak to laugh nervously, tells her, 'Jewel you must never listen to this.'"[127] Not only that but: "You should destroy it . . . Because it will be the white elephant in your room all your life."[128] The animal rears its head once more, or rather two metaphorical animals kiss each other: *the white elephant* and *the elephant in the room*.

A white elephant is "an object . . . considered to be with-out use or value." It likely originated "from the story that the kings of Siam . . . were accustomed to make a present of one of these animals to courtiers who had rendered themselves obnoxious." Herzog's meaning is closer to the proverbial *elephant in the room*, "a significant problem or controversial issue which is obviously present but ignored or avoided as a subject for discussion."[129] Like Melville's "whiteness of the whale . . . a dumb blankness full of meaning," Herzog's figure of "the white elephant in your room" connotes both incomprehensibility and immensity.[130] Its presence in a human-sized room suggests physical danger and what Kant calls monstrosity ("An object is monstrous if by its size it destroys the purpose which constitutes the concept of it"[131]). This echoes the seemingly incomprehensible monstrosity we saw evinced by Joseph Merrick's moniker, The Elephant Man. Herzog's mixed metaphor casts the lacuna at the center of his film both as a deceptive gift and as a surrogate for the monstrous animal making those inconceivable sounds on a muted videotape.

BEAR HEAD

Jewel Palovak's response to Herzog's portmanteau of bestial figures—"the white elephant in your room"—is incomprehension. Indeed, her face—cheeks still and slack, eyes glassy and wide—conjures the very blank stare that Herzog imputes to the bear in the passage with which I began this chapter. This blank stare speaks to nature's "overwhelming indifference," the "*negative* pleasures" of the sublime; it is also an uncanny mirror—to be "blank" is precisely what the sublime experience does *to* the *human* face. As Gilbert-Rolfe puts it, "a face can only be blank because it's an array of mobilities on a surface, the front part of the head as opposed to the head itself. The face is the place where the body inter-faces with everything its face faces."[132] Because all five senses lie arrayed on the surface of the human face, it is generally how we *perceive* that which creates the terror and pleasure of the sublime. Because the face is also the seat of expression, it is also where our sublime terror and pleasure *register*. If, in *Grizzly Man*, the animal's blank stare is an inscrutable terror, what do we make of the human's blank stare as a response to that terror?

Take Willy Fulton's description of his discovery of the couple's remains:

> Pretty nasty-looking bear that I had seen here before is just sneaking slow, with his head down. Just the mean-est-looking thing coming through the brush. So I jumped on the airplane real quick and untied it. And took off. Turned around, flew over camp there. Just looked down and saw a human rib cage that I knew had to be either Tim or Amie laying there. And he was just eating that . . . So I circled around again. Got really low, and tried to run him off. Just over and over again with the airplane. Every time I would come over, he'd just start eating faster

and faster and crouch over this rib cage there. And right at that time, I just realized, "Wow! I was pretty close to getting eaten myself" is what I thought. And this shot of adrenaline like I've never had just came over me. And my throat went . . . couldn't breathe. My face went numb. My arms and legs went numb.

Fulton's response to his encounter with death resonates with the coroner's description of the effect of "the visual input of seeing a detached human being": "makes my heart race, makes the hair stand up on the back of my head." In both cases, the human head is like an electrified sensing organ— "my face went numb"; the "hair stand[s] up."

Meanwhile, Herzog's camera lingers on the blank expressions on the faces of these men after their testimonies: "after the coroner finishes recounting the graphic death tape, there is a long pause where Herzog chose to keep the camera on him after he was done talking—he could have ended the shot when he stopped speaking."[133] The shock to the system—as if the men are jolted to life by the presence of death—is visually conveyed through stillness and blankness. The body freezes, the mind is voided. Proximity to any abyssal absence—be it nature, death, or death by nature—effects in the perceiving mind a vertigo, a dizzying syncope, a blanking out of consciousness. The imagination "faints and vanishes," "sinks back into itself."[134]

Suggesting both the galvanic and gaping aspects of awe,

Fulton's "Wow!" echoes Palovak's when the coroner gives her Treadwell's still-ticking watch: "Wow! I can't even believe it!" "Wow!" isn't really a word. It's an ejaculation, probably imitative in origin, an oddly contagious open-mouthed gasp. It repeats Treadwell's own language about the bears' large size ("He's a big bear! A very big bear! Wow!"), threatening bodies ("It's really cool. And it's very serious"), and physical prowess: "Extremely emotional, extremely powerful . . . Amazing."

This is the argot of adventure sports. Treadwell was an avid rock-climber ("I've almost fallen off a cliff!") and a wannabe surfer. We hear more about Treadwell's "radical" lifestyle when Herzog interviews his parents and friends back in Florida. Treadwell attended college on a diving scholarship until he injured his back; used drugs off and on; worked on a cruise ship; went to California to try his hand at acting, losing the bartender part on *Cheers* to Woody Harrelson; body-surfed with a Union Jack boogie board; and invented an Australian accent and backstory. This last tidbit suggests that Treadwell was modeling himself on adventure gurus like *The Crocodile Hunter*, Steve Irwin, who also met an untimely death on nature's spike.

Amanda du Preez cites this kind of hobby and lifestyle as examples of "contemporary cultures of the extreme." Du Preez notes that these cultures wish to *immerse*: "Terror is no longer kept at bay but now overwhelms, overtakes and almost drowns the subject."[135] Paradoxically, this *deepening* into the sublime is often castigated as shallow: "contemporary thrill culture . . . drives to collapse the distinction between object and subject, in order to experience the sublime firsthand. The effect of this collapse is a flattened, commodified, and even kitsch sublime."[136] But I would suggest that thrill culture's "mindless pleasures" are actually not so far from Kant's lofty "clearing of the mind." The word "awesome," for instance, has persisted, though we now associate it with "surfer-dudes" or "airheads" (an aptly blank moniker).

There's a genre of the contemporary extreme sublime in film, from Kathryn Bigelow's *Point Break* (1991) to the documentary *Free Solo* (2018). To me, the paragon of this "surfer-dude" sublimity is the face of the young Keanu Reeves, his lapidary skin backlit by a kind of radiant awe. Reeves has famously played "airhead" characters like Ted from *Bill & Ted's Excellent Adventure* (1989) and Johnny Utah from *Point Break*. The film critic Angelica Jade-Bastién refers to Reeves's "transfixing stillness," echoing Bret Easton Ellis's comment that Reeves has a "stillness, an awkwardness even, that is unusually empathetic. He is always hypnotic to watch." Jade-Bastién compares him to Greta Garbo for his "immense screen presence,"[137] to which we might add a shared androgyny and what Roland Barthes called a divine "Essence":

It is not a painted face but a face in plaster, protected by the surface of its shadows and not by its lineaments; in all this fragile and compact snow, only the eyes, black as some strange pulp but not at all expressive, are two rather tremulous wounds. Even in its extreme beauty, this face is not drawn but instead sculptured into something smooth and friable, which is to say both perfect and ephemeral, matches somehow Charlie Chaplin's flour-white complexion, those vegetally dark eyes, his totemic visage.[138]

The emphatic paleness of Garbo's face in Barthes's description isn't incidental—sublimity is often connected with not just blankness but whiteness both literal (snow, cliffs) and racial. But though Barthes calls it the "archetype of the face," it remains uncanny. It has the face-as-object quality we saw in Janet Leigh's "porcelain skin" and the vegetal pulpiness of William Treves's description of The Elephant Man's face. But what makes this kind of face most strange is the quality of blankness, the lack of change which is still somehow expressive: "the mask is merely the addition of lines."[139]

The blank sublime of the airhead's face dilates time so that expression itself becomes a chasm—the eyes as wounds. But it opens out into absurdity as well—Chaplin's totemic visage always hovers on the brink of the silly, the dopey, the goofy. One interviewee in *Grizzly Man* compares Timothy's face to a cartoon: "He had this Prince Valiant haircut. And he could surf and go under water, and yet still that hair would hide that receding hairline. It was the most amazing thing I've ever seen. No matter how rough the surf, you never saw Timmy's forehead." Herzog here cuts briefly to

Treadwell speaking into the camera like it's a talking mirror: "How's the hair look?" Treadwell's self-consciousness about his appearance is obvious in the film: he plays with his hair, fiddles with his rainbow of bandanas, keeps his eyes hidden behind sunglasses.

At one point, he encounters what he perceives as a threat: "Boulders piled up and a happy face indelibly painted into the rock, like, looking at me. Very, very frickin' frightening huh? Whoever put it there knew what they were doing. It's a warning." The happy (or smiley) face—blank, frozen, framed, positive—would seem the perfect symbol of the surfer-dude culture Treadwell embraced. But perhaps it hits too close to home, an uncanny mirror of the face he always wore like a mask of happiness, awe, and wonder. This is the risk of the blank sublime: that it will absorb all feeling, all relation. This can go two ways. Either you're so paralyzed with fear that you become insensible to others, solipsistic. Or, a lofty pathos flips into the pits of bathos. *Grizzly Man* is about death but it tempts us to laughter.

Whenever I spend time dwelling on the film, my mind fills with that koan-like nonsense rhyme:

Algy met a bear.
The bear met Algy.
The bear was bulgy.
The bulge was Algy.[140]

Even the moments of comedy in the film bespeak death. Treadwell mourns the death of a bee with a redundant simile—"It was working, busy as a bee, and it died right there. It's beautiful, it's sad, it's tragic"—until he realizes it's alive: "Well, the bee moved. Was it sleeping?" Herzog asks Palovak if she considers herself Treadwell's widow; she scoffs, fully cracks up, then abruptly replies in all apparent seriousness: "Yeah, you know in some ways I do."

The pleasures of humor and the pleasures of the sublime can placate our losses, but they can't truly compensate for them. They can't help us mourn. While some glibly postulate that Treadwell was "asking for it," we can't say the same of his companion in death. As Herzog says of Treadwell's true widow, his girlfriend at the time, Amie Huguenard: "we never see her face. Here it is obscured by her hands and her hair . . . The second shot that we have doesn't show her face either. She remains a mystery veiled by a mosquito net, obscured, unknown." As ever, the voice-over protests too much.

Far more effective and heartbreaking is the footage Herzog shows us late in the film: Huguenard drifting in and out of the frame, ducking, presumably to preserve Treadwell's illusion—that he was "alone" with the bears. She's watching a bear at the top of a stream, the one whose face Herzog tries and fails to read:

Is Amie trying to get out of the shot? Did Treadwell wait till his last tape to put her in the film? And what haunts me, is that in all the faces of all the bears that Treadwell ever filmed, I discover no kinship, no understanding, no mercy . . .

We see them juxtaposed: the obscured human face, the blank animal face, reminding us that not everything was on camera, not everything is within our compass.

Treadwell's father describes the moment he knew his son was dead: "she was sitting on the edge of the bed, staring at the television, and I saw Timmy's face. I hadn't heard the sound or the news yet, but I knew just by seeing Timmy's face on TV and hearing my wife's reaction, that the worst had happened." In vain, we imagine the face on the screen, a mother's reaction, the shock of grief indexed but unspoken. This is the horror we keep at bay with goofiness, play, euphemism, metaphor, sublimity—with a dumb blankness full of meaning.

5.

E-

FACED

WORD OF THE YEAR

In 2015, the *Oxford English Dictionary*'s Word of the Year (WOTY) wasn't a word at all:

This image is technically known as the "Face with Tears of Joy" emoji.[141] The press release on the OED Blog was rather self-congratulatory about this oxymoronic WOTY:

> That's right—for the first time ever, the Oxford Dictionaries Word of the Year is a pictograph: . . . the 'Face with Tears of Joy' emoji . . . There were other strong contenders from a range of fields . . . but [Face with Tears of Joy] was chosen as the 'word' that best reflected the

ethos, mood, and preoccupations of 2015. Why was this chosen? Emojis (the plural can be either *emoji* or *emojis*) have been around since the late 1990s, but 2015 saw their use, and use of the word *emoji*, increase hugely . . . Emojis are no longer the preserve of texting teens—instead, they have been embraced as a nuanced form of expression, and one which can cross language barriers.[142]

This explanation is stuffed with overcompensation. The choice to use an emoji is defended on the grounds of relevance, popularity, adult use, nuance, and portability across languages. Note the tension between these last two justifications: nuance suggests an almost finicky desire to pinpoint an exact meaning, while crossing language barriers implies a kind of universality.

This is a familiar tension in how we feel about language—it is incorrigibly slippery; it is the basis of understanding—but it also speaks to a tension about faces. The emoji—by which I mean the basic alphabet of variations on the happy face—epitomizes this tension because it is both a sign and a face. On one hand, we can trace the emoji to a history of attempts to perfect language by using the authenticity, transparency, intentionality, and legibility we assume of The Ideal Face. On the other hand, in current practice, the emoji is simply an extreme case of the slipperiness and hollowness that characterize signs as such and make them available for play. It is an adamantly material, quasi-facial sign with distinctive uses, dimensions, temporalities, and effects.

A BRIEF HISTORY

An *emoji* is an *ideogram* or a *pictogram* or a *pictograph*: all four words are portmanteaus that gesture toward a long history of efforts to merge two different forms—pictorial and linguistic—in order to improve communication. One origin of emoji is punctuation, often linked to a largely nonverbal medium: music. As Theodor W. Adorno notes in his charming essay "Punctuation Marks," a punctuation mark taken in isolation acquires a "definitive physiognomic status of its own, an expression of its own."[143] In 1881, the American satirical magazine *Puck* used punctuation marks to create a new "typographical art" that would "lay out . . . all the cartoonists that ever walked":[144]

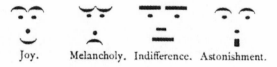

Joy.   Melancholy. Indifference. Astonishment.

Thirty years later, Ambrose Bierce proposed "the snigger point, or note of caccination"—an upturned horizontal parenthesis would represent "a smiling mouth." Introducing the first of many calls for ways to signal irony, Bierce wrote that the snigger point ought to be "appended to every jocular or ironical sentence."[145] And in a 1936 *Harvard Lampoon* article, Alan Gregg proposed (-) for a smile, (--) for a laugh ("more teeth showing"), (#) for a frown, and (★) for a wink.[146]

In his "Lectures on Aesthetics," delivered at Cambridge in the late 1930s, Ludwig Wittgenstein claimed that the problem with linguistics at the time was a focus on "the form of words" rather than "the use made of the form of words." If language is actually an activity, like talking, writing, traveling on a bus, and so on, then we can aim to *do* it better. For Wittgenstein, this meant making language more precise, more apt to capture feelings and character: "One thing that is intensely important in teaching is exaggerated gestures and facial expressions," he said. "The word is taught as a substitute for a facial expression or a gesture." He went on:[147]

10. If I were a good draughtsman, I could convey an innumerable number of expressions by four strokes—

Such words as 'pompous' and 'stately' could be expressed by faces. Doing this, our descriptions would be much more flexible

I assume that Wittgenstein wrote these proto-emoji up on some kind of board. But, given that the published lectures were compiled from the class notes of multiple students, I wonder how exact these drawings are, and which of these faces is meant to signify "pompous" and which "stately."

In 1969, Vladimir Nabokov made a similarly pompous and stately claim for the precision and flexibility of a pictogram. To the admittedly absurd question, "How do you rank yourself among writers (living) and of the immediate past?" he replied: "I often think there should exist a special typographical sign for a smile—some sort of concave mark, a supine round bracket, which I would now like to trace in reply to your question."[148] Why not just smile then, Uncle Vlad? Well, because this interview was not, in fact, in person. Nabokov insisted on conducting most of his interviews by letter, so keen was he not to speak "off the Nabo-cuff," as he put it.[149]

Wittgenstein and Nabokov both brainstorm pictograms when prompted by a question about *aesthetic* judgment. But the turn to the typographical aims for something closer to a clear expression of *emotion*—something more "flexible and various," "some sort of . . . mark"—one that will be immediately understood, that is generalizable, that is in fact *better* than language. This punctuational compulsion leads directly to contemporary rhetoric about the emoji's capacity to cross generational, geographical, and linguistic lines.

The second lineage for present-day emoji—the smiley face—emerged in the 1960s, once again capitalizing on our faith in the face as a universal sign. In 1963, State Mutual Life Assurance Company of Worcester, Massachusetts hired an American commercial artist named Harvey Ball (I'm not making that up) to create a happy face "to raise employee morale." Ball spent ten minutes and State Mutual Life Assurance spent $45 on the design: a bright yellow background, black oval eyes, and a full smile. It was imprinted on more than fifty million buttons.[150] Philadelphia brothers

Bernard and Murray Spain were responsible for popular-
izing it as "the happy face." In 1970 they seized on it for
a campaign to sell novelty items—buttons, mugs, t-shirts,
bumper stickers—emblazoned with the symbol and sometimes accompanied by the phrase "Have a happy day," which
eventually mutated into "Have a nice day." A Frenchman
named Franklin Loufrani legally trademarked this design as
the "Smiley" in 1972. Although it came before the digital
revolution, the cartoony simplicity of this iconic grapheme
influenced the aesthetic of both the emoji and its on-screen
precursor, the emoticon.

This last is the third lineage of the emoji. The word *emoticon* is a portmanteau of *emotion* and *icon*. Wikipedia defines it
as "a pictorial representation of a facial expression using characters—usually punctuation marks, numbers, and letters—to
express a person's feelings or mood, or as a time-saving meth-
od."[151] On September 19, 1982, Scott Fahlman of Carnegie
Mellon proposed the first digital emoticons on a computer
science message board:[152]

```
19-Sep-82 11:44    Scott E  Fahlman            :-)
From: Scott E  Fahlman <Fahlman at Cmu-20c>

I propose that the following character sequence for joke markers:

:-)

Read it sideways.  Actually, it is probably more economical to mark
things that are NOT jokes, given current trends.  For this, use

:-(
```

The need for a form of punctuation adequate to the inflections of tone here is keyed, like Bierce's snigger mark and Nabokov's supine bracket, to the effort to signify irony.

While the original emoticons stood sideways, a new horizontal format appeared in 1986, like this: (*_*). *Kaomoji* emerged with the American Standard Code for Information Interchange, or ASCII NET. Kaomoji use carrots, asterisks, dashes, underscores, and parentheses to create faces that can be perceived without (imagining) tilting your head. Often confused with emoji, kaomoji are strictly text-based, about a decade older than emoji, and etymologically distinct. The word *kaomoji* combines two words in Japanese, *kao* (face) and *moji* (character), while the word for image-based *emoji* combines the words *e* (picture) + *moji* (character). (This means, by the way, that the *e-* in *emoji* has nothing to do with the electronic prefix *e-* in *email* nor with the affective prefix *emo-* in *emoticon*.)

In the late 1990s, the Japanese phone company, DoCoMo i-mode, noticed that mobile users were increasingly using picture messages, which are much larger files than text messages. DoCoMo's Pocket Bell pagers were especially popular because they had the capacity to send a heart symbol. When a business-oriented pager was released that dropped the heart, there was an outcry among users, some of whom abandoned the company. To draw them back, DoCoMo engineers designed a set of commonly used pictures that could be added to text messages. Their innovation was to make each image into a single character, crucial because text messages at the time had character limits of 60-140.

The transition from emoticon to emoji was in some ways more profound than that from punctuation mark to emoticon. Emoticons and emoji are both character forms but most emoticons, whether vertical or horizontal, essentially represent a face, while the content of emoji ranges widely because they are just tiny pictures. This is the original set of 176 emoji, just acquired by the Museum of Modern Art in New York:

Explaining the design of this first set, one of the inventors, Shigetaka Kurita, makes a claim for the emoji's directness and universality:

The introduction of the iPhone, whose users all have access to the same stock of emoji, has definitely been a great help. If they had continued to develop differently depending on the device, then I don't think they would have become as ubiquitous.

I don't accept that the use of emoji is a sign that people are losing the ability to communicate with words, or that they have a limited vocabulary. Some people said the same about anime and manga, but those fears were never realised. And it's not even a generational thing . . . People of all ages understand that a single emoji can say more about their emotions than text . . . I accept that it's difficult to use emoji to express complicated or nuanced feelings, but they are great for getting the general message across.[153]

Kurita also predicts that emoji will naturally progress toward greater specificity: "I think the next step for emoji will be more localisation. There are already lots of symbols that are specific to Japanese culture and society, and I expect the same to happen in other countries."[154]

Once again, we see a tension between "getting the general message across" and "more localisation . . . symbols that are specific to" a particular "culture and society." As it turns out, you can try to "humanize" communication by putting a "face" to it, or "universalize" communication with iconography, but either way, you can't escape the contradictory logic of both signs and faces. The emoji—and the emoticon, the smiley face, and the punctuational pun before it—may *promise* immediacy, specificity, and clarity of intention. But in effect they suffer the distortion and drift of all figures.

EMOJI DRIFT

You can see this perpetually shifting ground even in our most popular emoji. Take the emoji 😱 ("Face Screaming in Fear"), defined this way on iEmoji.com:

> Overwhelming fear, surprised probably pale afterwards, scare tactics . . .
>
> iEmoji old name: About to scream, depressed . . .
> Unicode note: Shocking (like Edvard Munch's "The Scream")

The multiplicity of its origins has led it to develop in rather unexpected directions:

The Scream   *Shock*   *Face Screaming*   *Scared Cat*
                                       in Fear

"Face Screaming in Fear" is a riff on the popular "shock" emoticon. When this developed into an Apple emoji, it ended up incorporating an allusion to Edvard Munch's painting *The Scream* (1893). And its most recent version has subsumed the internet's ubiquitous obsession with cats. While it works all the time in context—it functions—we are very far indeed from the idea that this specific emoji expresses one person's emotion or saves communicative time.

Another example is 😂, the "Face with Tears of Joy" emoji and the OED 2015 WOTY. Once upon a time, the emoticon XD was used to convey a face guffawing with its mouth open and its eyes closed—a visual version of LOL, or "laughing out loud." The punctuation-based emoticon :'-) was used in a similar vein. But these three versions of cracking up are not equivalent to each other in meaning, not to mention tone: on Reddit, XD, and its phonetic transcription *ecks dee*, is considered a form of sarcastic "shitposting." Rather than resolving this kind of ambivalence, however, we tend to intensify it:

LOL → LOLOL → LULZ
:) → :D → XD → XDDD
😀→😄→😆→😂→😂😂😂

They all entail repetition—a vestige of language's limited capacity for intensification—but these three progressions toward "laughing very hard" each operate with a different logic. There's the bizarre semantic distortion of LOL into LOLOL—laughing out loud out loud—then into LULZ, ironically a homonym of "lulls." The staggered repetition of XD into XDDD, which almost animates the letter D into a laughing mouth, makes a bit more sense but still weirdly multiplies only the mouth and not the eyes.

You'd think 😂, affectively intense and concise, would

have improved clarity while eliminating the need to repeat altogether. But, according to a recent study, some interpret the OED's 2015 WOTY as positive, while others interpret it as negative. Unlike its predecessor emoticons and acronym, users are in fact split on whether this emoji means "laughing so hard I'm crying" or "crying through my laughter."[155] Despite recent attempts to render emoji more life-like, which aim to make emoji visually precise while still skirting the uncanny and grotesque effects of hyperrealism, we still love to repeat 😂.[156] In other words, even as we move ever closer to a lively or clear face in the emoji, it is still just as slippery as language.

Consider one medium where emoji are commonly used: instant messaging on GChat, iMessage, and Facebook Messenger. According to *The New York Times*, a 2014 study at Yeshiva University found that "when researchers [swapped] two unrelated instant-message conversations, as many as 42 percent of participants didn't notice."[157] You'd think emoji would improve things, as they put a face to the meaning and the moment of messaging. An NPR article observes:

Emojis were supposed to be the great equalizer: a language all its own capable of transcending borders and cultural differences. Not so fast, say a group of researchers who found that different people had vastly different interpretations of some popular emojis. The researchers published their findings for GroupLens, a research lab based out of the Department of Computer Science and

Engineering at the University of Minnesota, Twin Cities. "I think some people thought that they could use [emoji] with little risk and what we found is that it actually is at high risk of miscommunication," one researcher said.[158]

This kind of miscommunication gets worse when we send text messages across platforms. Just look at how much angrier the "Thinking Face" emoji looks on a Samsung Galaxy 🤔 than on an iPhone 🤔 —an effect due to the darkened eyes, inverted right eyebrow, and frownier mouth.

And as for transcending cultural differences, the last decade has seen a Civil Rights Act's worth of debate about the identity politics of emoji. Is emoji yellow face?[159] Why don't emoji include *all* the shades of skin and hair?[160] Why are certain workers depicted only as male?[161] Even after Apple rolled out a new range of options—blond and black; male, female, androgynous; old and young; a choose-your-own-ethnicity palette—new questions arose. Why can't emoji get black hair right?[162] What does it mean if you use an emoji shade darker than your own skin?[163]

Meanwhile, many emoji have drifted toward unintended meanings. The original Unicode name for 😤 was "Face With Look of Triumph" due to a Japanese cultural connotation. Because of how it was co-opted in the West, the Apple name for this emoji is now "Huffing with Anger Face." 😁 is called "Grinning Face with Smiling Eyes" but it's basically two eye-carets away from "Grimacing Face" 😬, which itself can be used to signal either distaste or awkwardness. 😵 was meant to convey dizziness but can mean shock or orgasm. 😎, "Smiling Face with Sunglasses," implies being out in the sun but means "being cool."

There's a whole subgenre of internet listicles and articles titled with some variation on "Emoji You're Using Wrong." This diversity of interpretation and connotation only grows when we combine emoji into sentences, as in this quiz (another subgenre) from *The New York Times*:[164]

1 Translate this emoji sentence:

My television is broken. I've been kicking it around like a soccer ball. I should call a repair man later.

I'm watching the World Cup. Call me later.

I don't usually watch television until after I browse the Internet, exercise and make my evening phone calls.

Can you watch the World Cup and talk later?

All of the above? This kind of quiz just emphasizes how fundamentally unstable emoji are: they tend inevitably toward misinterpretation and misconstrual, malapropism and mondegreen. Rather than serving as quick, efficient substitutes for words, emoji produce copious textual translations, as in a lengthy description of all the extant emoji in an essay in *The New Yorker*.[165] The essay's title ("I 💜 Emoji") itself begs the question: would you speak that as "I heart emoji" or as

"I love emoji"? Another article, "Do You Know What That Emoji Means?," both translates emoji into words *and* offers multiple definitions for them, occasionally insisting on one over the other as the "real" or "literal" meaning, as if that ever worked for human communication.[166]

Some neuroscience studies suggest that the human brain recognizes emoji as nonverbal communication—more like tones, gestures, and expressions than words. Other research shows that when we look at emoji, the same parts of our brain that respond to human faces light up; we unconsciously imitate and respond positively to them—we treat even a "sad face" emoji as a sign of "playfulness."[167] This haptic and affective bent to emoji does not make them any less of a language. Emoji—like concrete poems, pop art, and clichés—*are* signs; they're just signs that we play with rather than read, exactly.

A STACK OR STAGGER OF FACES

So, how *do* we play with these word-faces in our daily lives? For one, we rarely arrange emoji like words in a sentence nor do we fashion them into rebuses. In practice, we often *stack* them, pile them up on the screen. I'm sure we all have examples like this lurking on our phones:

This is the very first text message my then six-year-old nephew ever sent to me, before the predictive emoji feature and the advent of supersizing (the "blooming" effect you get when you use 1-3 emoji on an iPhone). First, he tries to use standard language (okay, adorable language), possibly with an effort to sign the sentiment with a face. But then, almost immediately . . . the stacking. I'd say that this is like a puppy pounding piano keys, were it not for his subsequent effort to use the emoji in a sentence ("I am doing ⚽") followed by . . . more stacking. I confess, I still have no idea what these messages meant. But my nephew's impulse toward repeating emoji as a way to convey emotion—and intensify it—came through loud and clear. My 💜 swelled to receive them.

The emoji in every platform (Apple, Google, Microsoft) are similar to one another—it's like they're in the same family, or as Lisa Gitelman puts it, the same "font"—and they seem to promise a universal range of expression. But the near-universal dislike for *The Emoji Movie* (7% on Rotten Tomatoes) and the outcry against the greater "realism" of emoji updates both suggest that we in fact perversely prefer our emoji inadequate, ambiguous, opaque. It's telling that when Apple gave us the option to "color" emoji racially (a laudable but Sisyphean task), they didn't apply this modularity to the most common ones: the primary set of smiley faces, the *ur*-moji, so to speak.[168] Honestly, I don't think we would want them to—for one, it would make the "yellow face" lurking behind emoji both more legible and more troubling.[169] And for another thing, I think we in fact enjoy seeing emoji in serial repetition, laid out in a tumbling grid down the screen, as browsable as the products on the shelf in a store or on the home page of a shopping search engine.

The emoji lends itself to stacking in part because it is *redundant*, in several senses of the word: it is easy to repeat, to recognize, and to replicate, and it's hardly ever indispensable. It also lends itself to stacking because, as I've suggested, it is as ambiguous as any other sign. That is, though emoji don't in fact allow for direct or transparent communication between users, they do spur a powerful desire to fondle that possibility. Our desire for emoji to convey true emotion or meaning comes up against their failure to do so. This yields an urge to repeat them. We compulsively tap those round buttons of feeling on the screen with a dispersed clitoral pleasure. This is, again, a kind of fetishistic play with tiny faces. Can the emoji speak? No. (Not yet, at least.) But we want it to. We fret at its face, as if its sheer repetition, its cumulative mass on the screen, will somehow make up for that inevitable impossibility of communication, will stack up some sense of how we really *feel*.

Because emoji thwart total comprehension, they become available for a particular kind of artistic play. When you Google "emoji art," a lot of kitschy mosaic-like works come up:[170]

This kind of art already suggests that the emoji tends toward synecdoche, a kind of pixel effect, and the full range of combination across vertical and horizontal axes. More interesting to me are creations like these literal emoji "cookies" or backformations like these messy emoji drawings:[171]

Here, the fact of emoji—emoji-ness—is more important than what each individual emoji means.

Emoji art doesn't try to make emoji "unique," "beautiful," "sublime," or "new." Rather, it tends to play with context, framing, media, puns, repetition, and dilation. In this sense, it probably belongs to the Pop Art family. The best pieces of emoji art I've seen play with the stacking I noticed in my nephew's texts, but also with a kind of *staggering*: a shifty, staccato form that results in skewed, overlapping, and flickering effects.

The artist Yung Jake has been using the emoji paintbrush tool, emoji.ink, to make distinctively twenty-first century portraiture.[172] As *Vice* magazine puts it, Yung Jake uses emoji ink "to transform music notes into Kim Kardashian's hair, envelopes into Wiz Khalifa's teeth, and 'index pointing up' emoji into the *Seinfeld* creator's chin."[173] Yung Jake's work reminds me of Andy Warhol's renditions of celebrities, Roy Lichtenstein's paintings of comics, and Chuck Close's late dilated-pointillist portraits.[174] Yung Jake tweaks the queerness and consumption of hip hop, incorporating french fries, cookies, cherries, and kiss marks into a portrait of Beyoncé[175]:

The stacking of emoji achieves its ironic apogee here, as the form's tendency toward repetition is both alluded to and distorted through an overlapping effect like roof tiles or playing cards. This corresponds visually to our experience of looking at/reading the emoji in these paintings, too. We shuffle between meanings as we zoom in: Is Beyoncé as sweet as cookies and cherries, as addictive as french fries, or are these simply the best emoji to capture the shades of her face? Is Jake making a celebration or a critique or a joke of our desire to consume her (as per the rumor that Sanaa Lathan bit her chin at a party)?[176] Is Beyoncé made of kisses or does she compel our kisses and would this many kisses blur her features like the touch of a million lips to an icon?

The visual stutter here suits the halting and, again, masturbatory rhythm of new online media forms like the GIF. Meaning grows skittish—or maybe pops and locks. We don't use emoji to create meaning like a sentence, qualify meaning like punctuation, or bestow meaning with emotional intention. Instead, we stack and stagger emoji, sparking brief bursts of emotional intensity and interpretive pleasure, which both derive precisely from the emoji's essential ambiguity.

THE POLITICS OF EMOJI

In her essay, "Visceral Abstractions," Sianne Ngai asserts that the birth of the smiley face in "the golden age of capitalism" was no accident: "The smiley face . . . expresses the face of no one in particular, or the averaged-out, dedifferentiated face of a generic anyone. It calls up an idea of being stripped of all determinate qualities and reduced to its simplest form through an implicit act of 'social' equalization, or the relating of each and every individual face to the totality of all faces." This makes the smiley, she argues, "an uncanny personification of the collectively achieved abstractions of the capitalist economy: abstract labor, value, capital."[177] Ngai cites the passage in *Capital* I discussed in relation to *Grizzly Man*, where Marx analogizes the general equivalent within a value system to "*the animal*" as an "individual incarnation of the entire animal kingdom."[178] Ngai confesses that the idea of a single abstract animal—The

Animal—sitting beside all the others gives her "the willies." The capitalist smiley stirs similar "visceral feelings": with its "unflinching gaze," it is "palpably unsettling" and "eerily abstracted" due to its "averaged out appearance."[179]

Why don't emoji produce these Gothic effects of shiver and disgust? Are they too id-like—more Animal from *The Muppets* than Marx's *the animal*? Or are they too bland? Emoji seem likelier to provoke boredom than discomfort—as per people's responses to *The Emoji Movie* or to this building in the Dutch City of Amersfoort:

This literal monument to emoji feels like that classic tell of urban gentrification: sponsored graffiti. It also spatializes emoji in an unfamiliar way. We are used to seeing emoji closer together, more of them in a row, or in staggered, Tetris-like stacks. Isolated from each other, staring out blankly at us, they seem a parody of the idea of a face-to-face encounter.

Architect Changiz Tehrani explains: "In classical architecture they used heads of the king or whatever, and they put that on the façade. So we were thinking, what can we use as an ornament so when you look at this building in 10 or 20 years you can say 'hey this is from that year!'"[180] But these are obviously not functional gutters, and while gargoyles are famously all different from one another, each emoji stares the same way down at us, emitting neither rainwater nor meaning nor feeling. If, as Tehrani says, "only faces were chosen as they were the most expressive and recognizable emoji," what do they express beyond the notion of expression?

For Ngai, the smiley is the perfect symbol of late capitalism's conformity, abstraction, and commodity production. I would argue that the emoji is the celebration of customized choice in contemporary neoliberal capitalism. That is, the emoji wears capitalism, too, just with a different skin—to use the term for how companies render each Unicode with their own personalized, and copyrighted, design.[181] Emoji is a commodity fetish. It relies on the purchase of an expensive item (a "smart phone") that obscures the often horrific labor practices that subtend its production. Emoji come with most smart phone platforms now, and there have been several spin-off products, like kaomoji and topic-specific emoji keyboards and apps. The popular Apple platform generates new emoji with every software update, from about 90 to 2,600 in the last decade, in response to petitions. Apple has tried to reduce our anxiety about an endless profusion of emoji with two features: "frequently used" and "predictive" emoji—the latter assumes that every word potentially has an emoji substitute, though the phone can't (yet) read your mind for what you wish to express.

Hence the *premoji*, my portmanteau of *premonition* + *emoji*: that feeling when you're hunting on your phone for an emoji that doesn't yet exist. You want to use it; it should be there; you feel sure you've seen it before. But you can't find it. It's the digital version—in both senses of the word—of something being on the tip of your tongue. If nineteenth-century free market capitalism is embodied in that phantom limb, Adam Smith's invisible hand of the market, then our current version of capitalism—with its pretense to total access, individual preference, and customization—is embodied in the premoji, the promise of everything at the tip of your finger.

The tension between individual and mass identity that Ngai sees in the capitalist smiley face ("the relating of each and every individual face to the totality of all faces") sits at the heart of the neoliberal emoji as well. But I think that, for now, this tension within the emoji is *live*—an active, flickering oscillation rather than a merging into uniformity. The staggered and stacked effects of emoji warp the time and logic of the free market from within, diverting us from its causal trajectories, ordered accumulation, and supposedly spontaneous, direct, and transparent emotions.

To be clear, the emoji does not *counter* capitalism's imperatives to produce, consume, and customize; rather, it draws our attention to their absurdity. This may just seem like that contemporary irony I noted as a possibility in Yung Jake's art—bad faith delectation in the hieroglyphs of commodity fetishism. And it may be just a matter of time before the emoji goes the way of the smiley—taking up its banal place in the land of *Forrest Gump* blockbusters and corny bumper stickers. But I find it interesting that when corporations or advertising or movies try to swallow emoji and spit them back at us, we tend to reject those efforts. We have been offered, and largely declined, for example, Ebroji and Homojis.[182] While giant Silicon Valley companies continue to diversify and monetize our portfolio of emoji options, we still harp on our favorites, repeat them to opacity, make them illegible to outsiders, and slip them into new contexts.

Beyond the sexualization of various fruit emoji (an old and storied way to duck censorship), black/queer communities have creatively adopted and adapted emoji: 👀 is "peep this" or "side eye"; 🐐 suggests the commenter is unfazed; 🐐 = goat = G.O.A.T. = Greatest Of All Time; ☕ can imply sipping your tea, again unfazed, or "that's the tea," i.e. the gossip (exchanged over tea since Jane Austen's days). Before the 2018 film *Black Panther* was granted its own emoji, Black Twitter appropriated the "Woman Gesturing No" emoji (🙅) to imitate the Wakanda salute.[183] A Twitter feed called @BlckPeopleEmoji appeared in 2013, with this emoji for an avatar: 🌑. The 500 or so tweets and retweets from this account essentially existed to point out that, at the time, the only emoji we could use for a black person was the "New Moon Face" emoji. Along the way, came a riff: 🌑 Mixed emoji, which while probably ineffective as a sign, hilariously parodies America's obsession with "the color line."

Signifyin' with tiny toons might seem a low bar to set for political change. But the ways marginalized communities adapt emoji undoubtedly enhance our capacity for expression. Rather than trying to fix the sign or the face—a la "Emoji You're Using Wrong"—these communities instead conjure genuinely novel terms for what Iris Murdoch called a "new vocabulary of attention" and a "new vocabulary of experience."[184] They continually turn the ambivalence of faces into an opportunity, even a kind of joy.

CONCLUSION

PROFILING

As I was finishing this book, a new app took social media by a storm. It was called Face App and it allowed you to age your face, to see what you would look like at fifty or at eighty years old. I never downloaded it, but from the screenshots that appeared on my timeline, the versions of one's face it spat forth seemed startlingly vivid, without falling on either side of the uncanny valley—neither too cartoonish nor too realistic. Within days, conspiracy theories cropped up. The company was Russian; the app was a cover; nobody was reading the terms and conditions; Face App was collecting faces. These fears may have been exaggerated, but they were not unfounded. The problem of the twenty-first century may well be the problem of the digital face.

It began with Facebook, founded in 2004 and named for the analog paper book that Harvard students used to identify one another, ostensibly to put together study groups, but actually for dating or, more likely, hooking up. The first version of the app, Facemash, was a "Hot or Not" ranking system for photos scanned from a set of online "face books" from different Harvard residential houses. This binary hot/not, yes/no model has continued to pervade the sociality of internet technology, from the thumbs up/thumbs down to the swipe left/swipe right.

Facebook's relationship to the book has faded—the visual logic of photographs and videos has taken over the site—but its relationship to the face seems to have intensified. Over the last couple of years, users have reported being asked to "upload a photo of yourself that clearly shows your face," purportedly to prove that you're not a bot. Many suspect that there is, again, data harvesting afoot here, as facial recognition programs are being tested by companies like Google, Microsoft, and IBM. The worry is that this data will be used to surveil or target specific people. We have already seen facial recognition technology being used this way—in China, for example. News about the protests in Hong Kong that began in 2019 emphasized the various measures protestors are taking to prevent being identified—from scattering lasers to knocking down cameras.

Privacy concerns aside, the political problems with facial recognition abound. Your face can be used to "dox" you—to locate you and disseminate information about your address, your job, and your affiliations. Your face can be stored and run through programs that adjust its expressions and speech patterns—even for words you've never uttered. Perhaps worst of all, your face could be *misidentified*, especially if you don't fit the data set on which these algorithms were built. Recent studies show that "when the person in the photo is a white man, the software is right 99 percent of the time. But the darker the skin, the more errors arise—up to nearly 35 percent for images of darker skinned women."[185] These errors cross some of the lines I've discussed in this book. Facial recognition technology, for instance, can mistake black men for each other, black women for black men, and black people for gorillas. The power of The Ideal Face doesn't just sway our cultural preconceptions; it actually sorts people into hierarchies enforceable by law and physical force. Police are already using facial recognition technology to identify suspects; U.S. security agencies are developing it for airports and borders.[186]

What is most disconcerting about this perhaps inevitable slide toward a surveillance state based on the face is that we, the people, have chosen it. Self-selected identity has become state-sponsored identification. Your elective profile is now used to profile you. To a certain extent, none of this is new: consumer culture, popular culture, and high art have all historically co-opted our fusiform area to their advantage. Sex sells; faces sell. What interests me is how this reiteration of age-old tensions about the face—*look at me/don't look at me*—changes once that face becomes digital currency. What sorts of play become available or precluded? Beyond political efforts to thwart it, how have we adapted, aesthetically, to facial profiling technology?

FACE PLAY

In one sense, responses to this technology, both positive and negative, have revolved around an old and familiar model of The Ideal Face: the idea that it represents identity, authenticity, transparency, truth. In an era of "fake news" and anonymous trolls, putting your face to your name and your words is seen as worthy, "say it to my face," the ultimate rejoinder. But I find it fascinating, then, that this idea of the digital face—as proxy for a real face—has emerged at the same time as a panoply of technologies designed to take "playing with faces" to another level.

Apart from the emoji which, as I've described it, we prefer to keep opaque and love to stack and stagger, we now have the capacity to apply a whole range of filters to digital images of our own faces. You can add or remove hair or makeup; you can change gender; you can layer your face with animal features, both realistic and cartoonish; you can merge your face with another person's; and most popular on the Face App, you can time travel by aging yourself.

Jia Tolentino argues that we are now in The Age of Instagram Face, a cyborgian amalgam forged by social media, plastic surgery, and the app FaceTune:

It's a young face, of course, with poreless skin and plump, high cheekbones. It has catlike eyes and long, cartoonish lashes; it has a small, neat nose and full, lush lips. It looks at you coyly but blankly, as if its owner has taken half a

Klonopin and is considering asking you for a private-jet ride to Coachella. The face is distinctly white but ambiguously ethnic—it suggests a *National Geographic* composite illustrating what Americans will look like in 2050 . . . 'It's like a sexy . . . baby . . . tiger,' Cara Craig, a high-end New York colorist, observed to me recently. The celebrity makeup artist Colby Smith told me, 'It's Instagram Face, duh. It's like an unrealistic sculpture. Volume on volume. A face that looks like it's made out of clay.'"[187]

This face might seem to be the contemporary reductio ad absurdum of The Ideal Face. But the shadows of the stranger faces in this book lurk here, in the Instagram Face's figural hybridity, racial ambiguity, clay-like sculptural thingliness, animal features, blank sublimity, eerie layeredness, and, of course, in its origin point and favored playground: the internet.

Some of these new face technologies handily work to mask or disguise the face—people use them to protect themselves from being identified by the state or by employers. Others seem suited to certain changes in how we engage with celebrity culture. But for the most part, they simply represent the apotheosis of my overarching claim in *Stranger Faces*: we love to play with faces, to make them into art.

The digital face that I find the most interesting in this regard is the GIF. The Graphics Interchange Format was invented in 1987. While it originated as an image format with a set of shifting colors in a palette, we mostly think of it now as a brief, looping clip of film or animation. It is a matter of some debate how to pronounce the acronym GIF—its inventors lean toward a soft *g* like the peanut butter brand Jif, but lay users seem to prefer a hard *g*. The oscillation between the two seems fitting for this oscillatory form. Apps like Vine and TikTok have advanced and perpetuated its use, but its natural habitat is on social media: Facebook, Twitter, and Instagram.

The standard GIF usually depicts a human face in motion: whether turning toward or away from the "camera," changing expression, shifting very slightly, or erupting—into a smile, into laughter, with a spit-take. These so-called "reaction GIFs" often accompany or are accompanied by text; they supplement a post or are captioned with language. They can feel like punctuation or ejaculation—an exclamation point, a question mark, the "snigger point" that Ambrose Bierce proposed or the "special typographical sign for a smile" that Vladimir Nabokov suggested.

Unlike the emoticons or emoji that emerged to fulfil those needs, a poster tends to use one GIF at a time, rather than stacking them up. The GIF does lend itself to a long, dialogic conversation, however. You'll find on Twitter entire threads made up of GIFs, some echoing each other, others offering opposed or qualifying reactions ("more like____"). Without the original post to which they are reacting, these alternating flickers of emotion can feel redundant or baffling. A GIF isn't more efficient than language. Indeed GIFs often induce flurries of interpretation or questions about whose face it is, or how and where it can be found.

To me, more than the emoji, more than even a filtered image of your own face, the GIF represents the furthest thing from The Ideal Face. The GIF isn't singular but plural, a kind of language, yet much less fixed than the alphabet of emoji for which additions must be petitioned. It is rarely a frontal view and is often in motion, distorted, exaggerated, sometimes animalistic. You do not address the face of the GIF, because rarely does a person use a GIF of their own face. Rather, it serves as a temporary mask, a momentary avatar for the person who posts it, who can be of a different race, ethnicity, class, gender, and ability entirely. And yet it *is* an encounter, a daily aesthetic experience that compels repeated watching—not just in the iterative instance of the click, but in any popular GIF's continued distribution and longevity as a recognizable meme over time. It is a supremely pleasurable form of face play.

BLACK FACE

The supposed glow, transparency, and distance from animality in The Ideal Face—as portrayed in Levinas's model, for instance—connotes racial whiteness. In this, too, the GIF is its polar opposite. Sianne Ngai argues that "exaggerated emotional expressiveness" can "function as a marker of racial or ethnic otherness in general." As Lauren Michele Jackson notes in an article on "digital blackface," this manifests in a particularly gendered way for GIFs:

> [Internet GIF search engine] Giphy offers several additional suggestions, such as "Sassy Black Lady," "Angry Black Lady," and "Black Fat Lady" to assist users in narrowing down their search. While on Giphy, for one, none of these keywords turns up exclusively black women in the results, the pairings offer a peek into user expectations. For while reaction GIFs can and do [evoke] every feeling under the sun, white and nonblack users seem to especially prefer GIFs with black people when it comes to emitting their most exaggerated emotions. Extreme joy, annoyance, anger and occasions for drama and gossip are a magnet for images of black people, especially black femmes.[188]

Black femmes tend not only to carry the weight of emotional labor online, but also to serve as the vents for the expression of emotions, from happiness to sadness and everything in between. To signify affect isn't necessarily to command respect or earn capital. And as Jackson explains, this trend follows uncomfortably from a long history of blackface in America—its appropriative violence and perpetuation of stereotypes.

But despite this troubling history, let us not dismiss the cultural dominance of the black femme face. A vast flock of black femme faces flutters across the field of the Internet: GIFs of *The Real Housewives of Atlanta*, Whitney Houston, Mariah Carey, RuPaul, Angela Bassett, Naomi Campbell, Viola Davis, Rihanna, Beyoncé, Keke Palmer. And of course, the black woman with the greatest affective range, plasticity, nuance, and exposure to her face—and the longest history of taking on American affective burdens—is Oprah Winfrey. Oprah turns and opens her hands ("what did I tell you?"); Oprah leans back into someone, the barest flinch reflecting her pleasure in what she's watching; Oprah spreads her arms, her yelling mouth wide with joy; Oprah dabs her eyes with white tissue; Oprah looks skeptical—a narrowed eye, a blink, a frown. Oprah is our reigning queen of the GIF.

My ham-handed descriptions of these GIFs are more mnemonic, more generic than their actual use, which is quite various and as subject to the play of irony—both dramatic and semantic—as that of any language. The GIF's relationship to an actual person is attenuated, if not irrelevant: people become known *as* Blinking GIF Guy, or And I Oop Girl. Add filmic effects—a rapid zoom in, a shuddering blur, a visual distortion—and these strange faces become stranger indeed.

One of my favorite GIFs—I had to do an internet search to replicate it below but I chose not to hunt for its biographical origin, which seems beside the point—is of a black woman with her eyes rolling back in ecstasy:

At some point, someone—again, I don't know who—elected to add a trippy filter to it to intensify the intended effect, which is, per the GIF's name, "Omg Wow Yes." This is a twenty-first century impressionist portrait, continuously looping from two to three dimensions.

This woman's beauty; her race, gender, class, or ability; her availability for a face-to-face interaction; her relationship to me and to the world; the time between now and whenever this clip was recorded, made into a GIF, and distorted for emphasis—none of this really matters to the effect of my encounter with it. Though I've never actively used this GIF as a reaction online, I see this woman's face all the time—a one-way gaze, as I doubt she's seen mine. This face isn't a mirror of my soul or a window into hers. It's a face set in motion by the force of a specific feeling, a specific moment—a *punctum*. It will never perfectly map onto whatever I'm feeling, nor does it pretend to. Rather it resonates with me, reverberates with an affective intensity set free from its bodily source. This strange, stranger's face can't be profiled or co-opted—not even by its original bearer, whom it just happened to flutter over, ripple through, with a deep and unaccountable pleasure.

NOTES

1   Sally Adee, "Specs that see right through you," *New Scientist* 2819 (July 5, 2011). "Sympathy, n." *Oxford English Dictionary*. Jonathan Cole, "Empathy Needs a Face," *Journal of Consciousness Studies* 8.5-7 (2001): 51-68.

2   Emmanuel Levinas, *Ethics and Infinity: Conversation with Philippe Nemo*, tr. Richard A. Cohen (Pittsburgh: Duquesne University Press, 1985), 86-7. *Totality and Infinity: An Essay on Exteriority*, tr. Alphonso Lingis (Dordrecht: KluwerAcademic Publishers, 1991), 50-51.

3   Several features of Levinas's idealized model of the face in his ethical philosophy have been subjected to critique: its whiteness, its maleness, its visibility/visuality, even its humanness. See Jacques Derrida "Violence and Metaphysics: An Essay on the Thought of Emmanuel Levinas," *Writing and Difference* (1967), tr. Alan Bass (Chicago: University of Chicago Press, 1978), 79-153; Barbara Ettinger, *The Matrixial Borderspace* (Minneapolis: University of Minnesota Press, 2006); and Barbara Ann Davey, "An Other Face of Ethics in Levinas," *Ethics and the Environment* 12, no. 1 (2007): 39-65.

4   Octave Mannoni, "Je sais bien, mais quand-même..." *Clefs pour l'imaginaire ou l'autre scène* (Paris: Editions du Seuil, 1969), 9-33.

5   William Pietz, "The Fetish I, II, and III," *RES: Anthropology and Aesthetics* 9, 13, and 16. Karl Marx, "The Fetishism of Commodities," *The Norton Anthology of Criticism and Theory*, eds. Vincent Leitch et al (New York: W.W. Norton, 2010), 776-783. Sigmund Freud, "Fetishism," *The Norton Anthology of Criticism and Theory*, eds. Vincent Leitch et al (New York: W.W. Norton, 2010), 929-952. For Pietz, the fetish is "proper to . . . a cross-cultural situation formed by the ongoing encounter of the value codes of radically different social orders" ("The Fetish I," 10-11). His anthropological account suggests that the threat of cultural relativism prompted the Western parties to describe Africans as "fetishists," animistic worshippers of idols and natural objects. Others have suggested that the Portuguese *feitico*, a charm, was actually a kind of proto-coin—a common currency that allowed exchange to take place between disparate economies. In either case, this story suits Marx's the-

ory of the fetish, in which the use-value of commodities gives way to their exchange-value; the labor that manufactured these objects is hidden in a system in which man-power of various kinds is leveled to one glowing marker of value: *money*, which has become naturalized to us as cash, coins, or mere numbers. For Freud, the sexual fetish—our most familiar use of the term—emerges during a primal scene when the young male first sees female genitals and becomes aware of castration as a possibility. The fetish object for which that boy reaches in that moment of panic, and to which he compulsively returns for pleasure or comfort, both acknowledges the (potential) loss of the (imagined) phallus and compensates or makes up for it. Apart from substitution and fungibility, we can trace other shared features of the anthropological, Marxian, and Freudian fetish: a spectral materiality; the objectification of persons and the animation of objects; and a liminal status between language and image. Pietz argues for other basic themes inherent to these three versions of the fetish: "irreducible materiality; a fixed power to repeat an original event of singular synthesis or ordering; the institutional construction of consciousness of the social value of things; and the material fetish as an object established in an intense relation to and with power over the desires, health, and self-identity of individuals whose personhood is conceived as inseparable from their bodies" ("The Fetish I," 10). Another crucial commonality for my argument is their shared paradoxical structure of *disavowal*, which combines recognition and denial, mourning and magical thinking.

6   Immanuel Kant, *Critique of Practical Reason* (1788), tr. Lewis White Beck (New York: MacMillan, 1989), 33.

7   Paul Bloom, "The Root of All Cruelty?" *The New Yorker* November 27, 2017.

8   Jennifer Egan, *Look at Me* (New York: Anchor, 2001), 3.

9   Egan, *Look at Me*, 4.

10   Egan, *Look at Me*, 5.

11   Cited in Stephen Lock, *The Oxford Illustrated Companion to Medicine* (New York: Oxford University Press, 2001), 651. Alice Hines, "How Many Bones Would You Break to Get Laid?" *New York Magazine*, May 28, 2019.

12   Egan, *Look at Me*, 6.

13   Egan, *Look at Me*, 42.

14   Egan, *Look at Me*, 43.

15   Immanuel Kant, *Critique of Judgment* (1790), tr. John Henry Bernard (New York: Barnes & Noble, 2005), 20-21.

16   Tim Vicary, *The Elephant Man* (Oxford: Oxford University Press, 2014).

17   Michael Howell and Peter Ford, *The True History of the Elephant Man: The Definitive Account of the Tragic and Extraordinary Life of Joseph Carey Merrick* (New York: Skyhorse, 2010), 115-116.

18   Howell and Ford, *The True History*, 118.

19   Quoted in Carly Findlay, "The Real and the Imagined History of the Elephant Man—seen as a viewer with a facial difference," *carlyfindlay. com.au*, August 12, 2017.

20   "The Autobiography of Joseph Carey Merrick" (1884). publicdomain-review.org.

21   Frederick Treves, *The Elephant Man and Other Reminiscences* (London: Cassell and Company, 1923), 1.

22   Akira Mizuta Lippit, "Magnetic Animal: Derrida, Wildlife, Animetaphor" *MLN* 113, no. 5 (December, 1998): 1111-1125.

23   Tilottama Rajan, *Deconstruction and the Remainders of Phenomenology: Sartre, Derrida, Foucault, Baudrillard* (Stanford: Stanford University Press, 2002), 48.

24   Treves, *The Elephant Man*, 4.

25   Treves, *The Elephant Man*, 3.

26   Treves, *The Elephant Man*, 5.

27   Treves, *The Elephant Man*, 10.

28   Works in disability studies about Joseph Merrick have focused on the ways in which ableism and medical discourse have perpetuated his mistreatment both as a human being and as a figure in artistic rep-

resentation. See Paul Anthony Darke's *The Cinematic Construction of Physical Disability as Identified Through the Application of the Social Model of Disability to Six Indicative Films Made since 1970* (The University of Warwick, dissertation submitted April 30, 1999) and his "*The Elephant Man* (David Lynch, EMI Films, 1980): An Analysis from a Disabled Perspective" *Disability & Society* 9, no. 3 (February 2007): 327–342; Fatimah Alzughaibi, "Exploring The Characters In The Elephant Man Through Two Disability Lenses," *International Journal of Science and Technology Research* 4, no. 9 (September 2015): 426–428; and Stanton B. Garner Jr., "In Search of Merrick: Kinesthetic Empathy, Able-Bodiedness, and Disability Representation" *Journal of Dramatic Theory and Criticism* 29, no. 2 (Spring 2015): 81–103.

29   Sigmund Freud, "The Uncanny," *The Norton Anthology of Theory and Criticism,* eds. Vincent Leitch et al (New York: W.W. Norton, 2010), 944.

30   Howell and Ford, *passim*, 73, 77.

31   Bernard Pomerance, *The Elephant Man: A Drama* (New York: Samuel French, 1979), 10.

32   Pomerance, *The Elephant Man*, 12.

33   This performance causes the actor a visibly physical pain that invokes, at least partially, what Merrick must have experienced—Pomerance says that "no-one with any history of back trouble should attempt the part of Merrick as contorted" (*The Elephant Man*, 7).

34   Bertolt Brecht, "On Chinese Acting," tr. Eric Bentley, *The Tulane Drama Review* 6, no. 1 (September, 1961): 130–136.

35   Pomerance, *The Elephant Man*, 4.

36   Martin Wainwright, "Antony and Cleopatra: coin find changes the faces of history," *The Guardian,* February 14, 2007. Photograph: Owen Humphreys/PA.

37   Sianne Ngai, *Ugly Feelings* (Cambridge: Harvard University Press, 2005), 91.

38   Aria Dean, "Poor Meme, Rich Meme," *reallifemag.com,* July 25, 2016.

39   Ngai, *Ugly Feelings*, 117.

40 Freud, "Fetishism," 955.

41 Walter Benjamin, "The Work of Art in the Age of Mechanical Reproduction," *The Norton Anthology of Theory and Criticism*, eds. Vincent Leitch et al (New York: W.W. Norton, 2010), 1173.

42 Julie Bosman, "Professor Says He Has Solved a Mystery Over a Slave's Novel," *The New York Times*, September 18, 2013.

43 Henry Louis Gates, Jr., "The Fugitive," *The New Yorker*, February 18, 2002.

44 Hannah Crafts, *The Bondwoman's Narrative* (New York: Warner Books, 2002), 162.

45 John Bloom, "Literary Blackface? The Mystery of Hannah Crafts," *In Search of Hannah Crafts: Critical Essays on The Bondwoman's Narrative*, eds. Henry Louis Gates, Jr. and Hollis Robbins (New York: BasicCivitas Books, 2004), 437.

46 Quoted in Williams, Adebayo, "Of Human Bondage and Literary Triumphs: Hannah Crafts and the Morphology of the Slave Narrative," *Research in African Literatures* 34, no. 1 (Spring 2003): 137.

47 John Stauffer, "The Problem of Freedom in *The Bondwoman's Narrative*," 53.

48 Celeste-Marie Bernier and Judie Newman, "*The Bondwoman's Narrative*: Text, Paratext, Intertext and Hypertext," *Journal of American Studies* 39, no. 2 (August 2005): 147-165.

49 See the story of James Williams in Ann Fabian's "Hannah Crafts, Novelist; or, How a Silent Observer Became a 'Dabster at Invention,'" *In Search of Hannah Crafts*.

50 Henry Louis Gates, Jr., "Introduction," *In Search of Hannah Crafts*, xxii-xxiii. Bernier and Newman, "*The Bondwoman's Narrative*," 158.

51 Bernier and Newman, "*The Bondwoman's Narrative*," 161.

52 "Authenticity, n." and "duplicity, n." *Oxford English Dictionary*.

53 Karen Sánchez-Eppler, "Gothic Liberties and Fugitive Novels: *The Bondwoman's Narrative* and the Fiction of Race," *In Search of Hannah Crafts*, 258.

54 Hannah Crafts, *The Bondwoman's Narrative* (New York: Warner Books, 2002), 5-6.

55 The one-drop rule is often thought of as a fact of the postbellum United States and it is true that it was only instantiated in law in the early twentieth century. The history of hypodescent and traceable blood in America, however, stretches back as far as the seventeenth century. See Christine B. Hickman "The Devil and the One Drop Rule: Racial Categories, African Americans, and the U.S. Census," *Michigan Law Review* 95, no. 5 (March 1997): 1161-1265.

56 As Zoe Trodd notes "So, like Douglass, Crafts recognizes the 'arbitrary relationship between a sign and its referent, between the signifier and the signified,' as Gates phrases the problem when discussing the 1845 Narrative." Trodd, "'Don't speak dearest, it will make you worse' *The Bondwoman's Narrative*, the Afro-American Literary Tradition, and the Trope of the Lying Book," *In Search of Hannah Crafts*, 298.

57 Crafts, *The Bondwoman's Narrative*, 117.

58 Crafts, *The Bondwoman's Narrative*, 27, 68, 94, 83.

59 Crafts, *The Bondwoman's Narrative*, 92. This distinction is maintained for those toward whom Hannah is feeling friendly as well: "I might, indeed, describe their size and figure, might enlarge on the color of their their eyes and hair, but after all what language could portray the ineffable expression of a countenance beaming with soul and intelligence?" (124). While face and countenance are congruent here, they are not always so allied: Mr Trappe's dark face, for example, is sometimes briefly blessed with a countenance hinting at kindness or pity.

60 Crafts, *The Bondwoman's Narrative*, 16.

61 Elaine Scarry, *Dreaming by the Book* (Princeton: Princeton University Press, 1999), 13.

62 Crafts, *The Bondwoman's Narrative*, 23.

63 Crafts, *The Bondwoman's Narrative*, 110, 27, 161.

64 Crafts, *The Bondwoman's Narrative*. See Dickson D. Bruce, Jr. "Mrs. Henry's 'Solemn Promise' in Historical Perspective," *In Search of Hannah Crafts*.

65   Crafts, *The Bondwoman's Narrative*, 56–57.

66   Crafts, *The Bondwoman's Narrative*, 148, 160.

67   Crafts, *The Bondwoman's Narrative*, 153.

68   Crafts, *The Bondwoman's Narrative*, 154.

69   Crafts, *The Bondwoman's Narrative*, 153.

70   Crafts, *The Bondwoman's Narrative*, 154.

71   Crafts, *The Bondwoman's Narrative*, 155.

72   Crafts, *The Bondwoman's Narrative*, 165.

73   Crafts, *The Bondwoman's Narrative*, 167.

74   Crafts, *The Bondwoman's Narrative*, 169, 165, 170, 203.

75   Crafts, *The Bondwoman's Narrative*, 205, 203–204, 211.

76   Crafts, *The Bondwoman's Narrative*, 210.

77   Crafts, *The Bondwoman's Narrative*, 212.

78   Crafts, *The Bondwoman's Narrative*, 213.

79   Henry Louis Gates, Jr. *The Signifying Monkey: A Theory of African-American Literary Criticism* (Oxford: Oxford University Press, 1988).Kevin Young, *The Grey Album: On the Blackness of Blackness* (Minneapolis: Graywolf, 2012), 24. Young writes of the *counterfeit tradition*, the "ways in which black writers create their own authority in order to craft their own, alternative system of literary currency and value, so to speak, functioning both within and without the dominant, supposed gold-standard system of American culture" (24). See also Young's book *Bunk: The Rise of Hoaxes, Humbug, Plagiarists, Phonies, Post-Facts, and Fake News* (Minneapolis: Graywolf, 2017).

80   Robin Wood, "Psycho," *Alfred Hitchcock's* Psycho*: A Casebook*, ed. Robert Kolker (Oxford: Oxford University Press, 2004), 79.

81   Alfred Hitchcock, *Psycho* (1960), United States: Shamley Productions and Paramount Pictures.

82   Raymond Durgnat, *A Long Hard Look at Psycho* (London: BFI, 2010), 50.

83   François Truffaut, *Hitchcock* (Simon and Schuster, 1985), 277.

84   Durgnat, *A Long Hard Look*, 16. The voice actors were Jeanette Nolan, Virginia Gregg, and Paul Jasmin.

85   Pietz, "The Fetish I, II, and III," *RES: Anthropology and Aesthetics* 9, 13, and 16. Marx, "The Fetishism of Commodities," *The Norton Anthology of Criticism and Theory*, 776-783. Freud, "Fetishism," *The Norton Anthology of Criticism and Theory*, 929-952.

86   Benjamin, "The Work of Art," 1176-77.

87   Gilles Deleuze, *Cinema One: The Movement-Image*, tr. Hugh Tomlinson and Barbara Habberjam (London: Continuum, 2005).

88   Quoted in Durgnat, *A Long Hard Look*, 18.

89   Durgnat, *A Long Hard Look*, 165.

90   Truffaut, *Hitchcock*, 272-3.

91   Truffaut, *Hitchcock*, 282-3.

92   Marx, "The Fetishism," 776.

93   Durgnat, *A Long Hard Look*, 153, 160.

94   Durgnat, *A Long Hard Look*, 150.

95   Courtesy of Universal Studios Licensing LLC, ©1960 Shamley Productions, Inc.

96   D.A. Miller, "Hitchcock's Hidden Pictures," *Critical Inquiry* 37, no. 1 (Autumn 2010): 115.

97   Miller, "Hitchcock's Hidden Pictures," 118.

98   Miller, "Hitchcock's Hidden Pictures," 114.

99   Miller, "Hitchcock's Hidden Pictures," 126-7.

100 Pietz, "The Fetish III," 109.

101 Courtesy of Universal Studios Licensing LLC, ©1960 Shamley Productions, Inc.

102 In his lecture on it, Vladimir Nabokov points out that there are really three personalities in Stevenson's novel: Jekyll, Hyde, and "the

Jekyll residue when Hyde takes over." *Lectures on Literature* (New York: Houghton Mifflin Harcourt, 1980), 183.

103 Levinas, *Totality and Infinity*, 140 (his italics).

104 Seth Friedman, "Misdirection in Fits and Starts: Alfred Hitchcock's Popular Reputation and the Reception of His Films," *Quarterly Review of Film and Video* 29 (2012): 89.

105 Werner Herzog, *Grizzly Man* (2005), United States: Lions Gate Films and Discovery Docs.

106 Marcus Bullock, "Watching Eyes, Seeing Dreams, Knowing Lives," *Representing Animals*, ed. Nigel Rothfels (Bloomington: Indiana University Press, 2002), 112.

107 Jeremy Gilbert-Rolfe, *Beauty and the Contemporary Sublime* (New York: Allworth Press, 1999), 114.

108 Quoted in Julie Kalil Schutten, "Chewing on the *Grizzly Man*: Getting to the Meat of the Matter," *Environmental Communication: A Journal of Nature and Culture* 2, no. 2: 193.

109 Charles Bell, *The Anatomy and Philosophy of Expression* (London: George Bell & Sons, 1877), 179. Charles Darwin, *The Expression of the Emotions in Man and Animals* (London: John Murray, 1872), 355.

110 Quoted in Jacques Derrida, *The Animal That Therefore I Am*, tr. David Wills (New York: Fordham University Press, 2008), 107-8.

111 Derrida, *The Animal*, 117.

112 Derrida, *The Animal*, 28.

113 Quoted in Sianne Ngai, "Visceral Abstractions," *GLQ: A Journal of Lesbian and Gay Studies* 21, no. 1 (January 1, 2015): 51.

114 Derrida, *The Animal*, 6.

115 Francis J. Gonzalez, "Moving Fragments," *Studies in Gender and Sexuality* 10, no. 2: 61.

116 Seung-Hoon Jeong and Dudley Andrew, "Grizzly Ghost: Herzog, Bazin, and the Cinematic Animal," *Screen* 49, no. 1 (Spring 2008): 8.

117 Schutten, "Chewing on the *Grizzly Man*," 198, 207, 204.

118 Freud puts it this way: "Faeces are the child's first gift, the first sacrifice on behalf of his affection, a portion of his own body which he is ready to part with, but only for the sake of somebody he loves." *The Complete Psychological Works of Sigmund Freud Vol. 17: An Infantile Neurosis and Other Works*, ed. and tr. James Strachey (London: Vintage Classics, 2001), 81. Jacques Derrida, *The Gift of Death*, tr. David Wills (Chicago: The University of Chicago Press, 1995).

119 Werner Herzog, *Herzog on Herzog*, ed. Paul Cronin (London: Faber and Faber, 2002), 81.

120 "Sublime, a. and n.," *Oxford English Dictionary*.

121 Gonzalez, "Moving Fragments," 61.

122 Arthur Schopenhauer, *The World As Will and Idea, Vol. I*, tr. R.B. Haldane and J. Kemp (London: Kegan Paul, Trench, Trübner, & Co., 1909), §39. Edmund Burke, *Philosophical Inquiry Into the Origin of Our Ideas of the Sublime and Beautiful* (London: W. & J. Neal, 1833), 65.

123 Schopenhauer, *The World As Will*, §39.

124 Kant, *Critique of Judgment*, 45.

125 Schopenhauer, §39.

126 Wallace Stevens, *The Collected Poems* (New York: Vintage, 1990), 131.

127 As David Johnson explains, the aesthetics of the scene are heightened by a "reality" or "indexical" effect: "this camera has been touched by Treadwell, which is now held by Palovak. Such tactile transference, if only imagined in the minds of viewers, is not unlike the sense of indexicality with which theorists of film realism invest the cinematic frame." Herzog's willful visual imposition of silence on Palovak and on the viewer affords a disavowal—we see that this recording exists, but all the same, we cannot hear it—that corresponds both to the cinematic illusion and to our human incomprehension of death. David T. Johnson, "'You Must Never Listen to This': Lessons on Sound, Cinema, and Mortality from Herzog's *Grizzly Man*," *Film Criticism* 32, no. 3 (Spring 2008): 76.

128 Jeong and Andrew call this an animetaphor that "does not serve as

a figure but rather leads to the extratextual animal beyond language" ("Grizzly Ghost," 6).

129 "Elephant, n." *Oxford English Dictionary*.

130 Herman Melville, *Moby-Dick* (London: St. Botolph Society, 1892), 186.

131 Kant, *Critique of Judgment*, 53.

132 Gilbert-Rolfe, *Beauty*, 117.

133 Schutten, "Chewing on the *Grizzly Man*," 205.

134 Jean-Luc Nancy, "The Sublime Offering," *Of the Sublime: Presence in Question*, ed. Jean-Francois Courtine, tr. Jeffrey S. Librett (Albany: SUNY Press, 1993), 43; Nancy quotes "sinks into itself" from Kant.

135 Amanda du Preez, "The Sublime and the Cultures of the Extreme: An Exploration," *Communicatio* 35, no. 2: 205.

136 Du Preez, "The Sublime," 206.

137 Angelica Jade-Bastién, "The Grace of Keanu Reeves," *Balder and Dash* February 9, 2016.

138 Roland Barthes, "Garbo's Face," *Mythologies*, tr. Annette Levers (New York: Hill and Wang, 1972), 73.

139 Barthes, "Garbo's Face," 73.

140 Quoted in Joseph T. Thomas, *Poetry's Playground: The Culture of Contemporary American Children's Poetry* (Detroit: Wayne State University Press, 2007), 43.

141 All emoji and their names and descriptions come from *emojipedia.org*.

142 "Word of the Year 2015," *Oxford Dictionaries*, November 17, 2015.

143 Theodor Adorno, "Punctuation Marks," *The Antioch Review 48*, no. 3 (1990), 300.

144 "Typographical Art," *Puck,* March 30, 1881, 65. Reprinted in Casey Chan, "The First Emoticons Were Used in 1881," *Gizmodo*, July 16, 2013.

145 Ambrose Bierce, "For Brevity and Clarity," *The Collected Work of Am-*

brose Bierce, XI: Antepenultimata (New York: The Neale Publishing Company, 1912), 387.

146 Alan Gregg, *The Harvard Lampoon* 112, no. 1 (November, 1936): 16, cited in Vyvyan Evans, *The Emoji Code: The Linguistics Behind Smiley Faces and Scaredy Cats* (New York: Picador, 2017).

147 Ludwig Wittgenstein, *Lectures & Conversations on Aesthetics, Psychology and Religious Belief* (Berkeley: University of California Press, 2007), 1.

148 Vladimir Nabokov, *Strong Opinions*, (New York: Vintage Books, 1973), 133-4.

149 Nabokov, *Strong Opinions*, 62.

150 Jimmy Stamp, "Who Really Invented the Smiley Face?" *smithsonian. com*, March 13, 2013.

151 *Wikipedia*, "Emoticon," accessed September 9, 2018.

152 "Original Bboard Thread in Which :-) Was Proposed," School of Computer Science Carnegie Mellon University.

153 Justin McCurry, "The Inventor of Emoji on His Famous Creations — and His All-Time Favorite," *The Guardian*, October 27, 2016.

154 McCurry, "The Inventor."

155 Eyder Peralta, "Lost In Translation: Study Finds Interpretation Of Emojis Can Vary Widely," *NPR*, April 12, 2016.

156 Caroline Cakebreak, "Here's how to use Apple's Animoji — the new talking emoji that has your voice and facial expressions," *Business Insider*, September 12, 2017.

157 Pamela Druckerman, "Decoding the Rules of Conversation," *The New York Times*, March 16, 2015.

158 Peralta, "Lost In Translation."

159 Caitlin Dewey, "Are Apple's new 'yellow face' emoji racist?" *The Washington Post*, February 24, 2015.

160 Monica Tan, "Apple adds racially diverse emoji, and they come in five skin shades," *The Guardian*, February 23, 2015.

161 Lizzie Plaugic, "Google's diverse emoji for women at work approved by Unicode Consortium," *The Verge*, July 14, 2016.

162 Samantha Sasso, "This New Emoji Is Getting Mixed Reactions On Twitter," *Refinery29*, December 14, 2017.

163 Kumari Devarajan, "White Skin, Black Emojis?" *NPR*, March 21, 2018; Andrew McGill, "White People Don't Use White Emoji," *The Atlantic*, May 9, 2016.

164 Simone S. Oliver, "Are You Fluent in Emoji?" *The New York Times*, July 25, 2014.

165 Hannah Goldfield, "I Heart Emoji," *The New Yorker*, October 16, 2012.

166 Marlynn Wei, "Do You Know What That Emoji Means?" *Psychology Today*, October 26, 2017.

167 Courtney Saiter, "The Psychology of Emojis," *The Next Web: Insider*, June 23, 2015; Christina Peréz, "To Emoji or Not to Emoji? The Real Message Those Little Icons are Sending," *Vogue*, April 25, 2017.

168 Colette Shade, "The Emoji Diversity Problem Goes Way Beyond Race," *Wired*, November 11, 2015.

169 Dewey, "Are Apple's."

170 Unattributed, *pinterest.com*.

171 Leslie Horn, "Emoji Cookies. I Repeat, Emoji Cookies," *Gizmodo*, November 28, 2012; Kathy MacLeod, "All the Emojis, Drawn," *The Hairpin*, March 27, 2013.

172 Guy Trebay, "Digital Artist Yung Jake Scores With Emoji Portraits," *The New York Times*, July 26, 2017.

173 Beckett Mufson, "Yung Jake's Emoji Portraits of Celebrities," *thecreatorsproject.com*, January 14, 2015.

174 Chuck Close, *James* (2002), oil on canvas, 276.23 cm x 213.36 cm, SF MoMA.

175 "Beyoncé" by Yung Jake, using emoji.ink.

176 Mara Siegler and Emily Smith, "Sanaa Lathan confirmed as star who bit Beyoncé," *Page Six*, March 30, 2018.

177 Ngai, "Visceral Abstractions," 40.

178 Ngai, "Visceral Abstractions," 51.

179 Ngai, "Visceral Abstractions," 35-36.

180 James Vincent, "This Building Uses Emoji Cast in Concrete as Modern Gargoyles," *The Verge*, April 24, 2017.

181 Lisa Gitelman, "Emoji Dick, or the Eponymous Whale," *Post45: Peer Review*, July 8, 2018.

182 Zeba Blay, "Jesse Williams Created A GIF Keyboard App, And It's Lit," *HuffPost*, January 22, 2016; Curtis Wong, "This 'Homoji' Keyboard Brings Queer Shorthand To Your Text Messages," *HuffPost*, February 16, 2017.

183 Jessica Saxon, "The definitive guide to what Black Twitter's favorite Emojis mean," *blavity.com*.

184 Iris Murdoch, "Against Dryness." *Existentialists and Mystics: Writings on Philosophy and Literature* (London: Penguin, 1997), 287-295.

185 Steve Lohr, "Facial Recognition Is Accurate, if You're a White Guy," *The New York Times*, February 9, 2018.

186 Robert Booth, "Police face calls to end use of facial recognition software," *The Guardian*, July 3, 2019.

187 Jia Tolentino, "The Age of Instagram Face," *The New Yorker*, December 12, 2019.

188 Lauren Michele Jackson, "We Need to Talk About Digital Blackface in Reaction GIFs," *Teen Vogue*, August 2, 2017.

ACKNOWLEDGMENTS

I wrote this book while at the University of California, Berkeley English Department. My thanks go to: Juliana Chow for organizing my 2009 English Graduate Association Colloquium, "Depth and Reflection," with Ashley Barnes; Wendy Xin for organizing the 2013 Consortium on the Novel panel, "Novelistic Legacies: Literary Criticism in the Age of Cinema," at which I delivered related talks. The members of the 2012 Contemporary Reading Group: Sarah Chihaya, Kathryn Fleishman, Eva Haberg, Lynn Huang, Sunny Xiang. The members of the 2012 English department junior faculty reading group: Todd Carmody, Kathleen Donegan, Nadia Ellis, Eric Falci, Catherine Flynn, David Landreth, Steven Lee, David Marno, Emily Thornbury. My other Berkeley colleagues who gave me feedback and suggestions: Charles Altieri, Stephen Best, Catherine Gallagher, Dorothy Hale, Karen Leibowitz, John Lurz, David Miller, Kent Puckett.

The Doreen B. Townsend Center for the Humanities for granting me a 2014-15 fellowship. The Hellman Fund, which sponsored the 2014 *About Faces* conference I organized with Andrea Gadberry. The participants of that conference: Elizabeth Abel, Glenda Carpio, Mary Ann Doane, Karen Glover, Jennifer Ham, Allyson Hobbs, David Lubin, Danny Marcus, Maura Nolan, Julie Orlemanski, Sharrona Pearl, Jill Richards, Rochelle Rives, Matthew Senior, Vanita

Seth, Santiago Slobodsky, Davide Stimilli. Participants of the Annual Comparative Literature Association conference panels at which I presented related talks: "Global v. Local Interartistic Borrowings" (2009), organized by Wendy B. Faris and Emma Kafalenos; "The Question of the Animal" (2010), by William C. Putnam; "*Prima Facie* and Second Nature: Prosopopeia and the Faces of Origin" (2012), by Andrea Gadberry and Amanda Jo Goldstein; "Graphic Reading" (2015), by Angus Brown and Charlotta Salmi. The University of California, Los Angeles English Department for inviting me to deliver the 2017 Kanner Lecture, "How to Read Faces."

Sarah Chihaya, Joshua I. Kotin, Kinohi Nishikawa, who organized The Contemporary Conference at Princeton where I delivered a talk about emoji in 2016, and who published a version of Chapter 5 as "😂: or, Word of the Year" in *Post-45: How to Be Now 2*, April 28, 2019.

Everyone at Transit Books, especially Adam Z. Levy for the keen editorial support and for believing that readers beyond the academy would be interested in these ideas.

Emily Brenes and Mike Isaac, who were my assistants via the Berkeley Undergraduate Research Apprentice Program when I first began writing this book in 2009, and whose deep research and sharp insights shaped it from the very start. *Stranger Faces* is dedicated to them.

NAMWALI SERPELL is a Zambian writer and Professor of English at Harvard University. She's a recipient of a 2020 Windham-Campbell Prize for fiction and the 2015 Caine Prize for African Writing. Her first novel, *The Old Drift* (Hogarth, 2019), won the 2020 Anisfield-Wolf Book Award for fiction, the 2020 Arthur C. Clarke Award for science fiction, and the *Los Angeles Times*'s 2020 Art Seidenbaum Award for First Fiction, and was named a *New York Times* Notable Book of 2019.

Undelivered Lectures is a narrative nonfiction series featuring book-length essays in slim, handsome editions.